TESTING TORNADO

Cold War Naval Fighter Pilot to BAe Chief Test Pilot

J. DAVID EAGLES AFC

The History Press

To my wife, Ann, for your help and necessary constant encouragement.

To the Royal Navy, for my education.

And to the memory of many friends lost along the way.

Cover illustrations: front: MRCA P02 flying at Mach 1.6/620kt on 13 June 1975; back: The author in MRCA prototype P02.

First published 2016

The History Press
The Mill, Brimscombe Port
Stroud, Gloucestershire, GL5 2QG
www.thehistorypress.co.uk

British Library Cataloguing in Publication Data.
A catalogue record for this book is available from the British Library.

ISBN 978 0 7509 6841 6

Typesetting and origination by The History Press
Printed and bound in Great Britain by TJ International Ltd

Contents

Foreword by Sir John Treacher KCB   4

1   Start Up   5

2   Australia   21

3   The Cold War   28

4   Empire Test Pilots' School   43

5   Boscombe Down   48

6   Buccaneer Front Line   67

7   Industry   73

8   EAP   131

9   Shut Down   136

Appendices

1   ETPS No. 22 Fixed Wing Course, Final Exam Paper   141

2   Typical Flight Test Report, C Squadron, Boscombe Down, January 1966   142

3   'Flying an 800-Knot Tornado'   144

4   Flight Test Report, EAP First Flight, 8 August 1986   154

5   'Test Pilot Involvement in Engineering'   157

Foreword by
Sir John Treacher KCB

I am pleased that David has decided to record his brilliant flying career, which was well and truly launched when his first squadron embarked in the aircraft carrier HMS *Victorious* in which I was serving at the time.

His natural ability was quickly recognised and he was soon selected for advanced training as an air warfare instructor and then for the Empire Test Pilots' School.

It was not long before British Aerospace realised his potential and the navy was happy to have him become chief test pilot of future developments.

Admiral Sir John Treacher KCB
Commander (Air) in David Eagles' first embarked squadron in
HMS *Victorious*; Captain of the aircraft carrier HMS *Eagle*;
retired as Commander-in-Chief, Fleet

1

Start Up

My flying career started in the library of Mirfield Grammar School, in the West Riding of Yorkshire, in the middle of 1953. I was studying Geology at A level but had become aware that I would have to join one of the services for national service, either before or after university. I began to consider which of the three services it should be and I came across two paperback books in that library. They were *Fleet Air Arm* and *Ark Royal*, published by the Ministry of Information in 1942 and 1943, and they were full of pictures of pilots in sheepskin-lined jackets leaning into the wind as they made their way up a heaving flight deck to man their fighters. I still have these books and they still give me the same feelings I had then: 'Where do I join?'

HMS
Indefatigable
in Portland
Harbour
during 1954.

After much letter writing, form filling and interviewing I arrived at the Naval Air Station at Lee-on-Solent and began the uncomfortable experience of becoming a naval airman 2nd class and a national service upper yardman. There were twenty of us in that intake and after a week of kitting out and square-bashing we joined the Fleet Carrier HMS *Indefatigable* in Plymouth.

Indefat, still bearing the scars of a kamikaze attack from her time in the Pacific nine or ten years earlier, was now a floating classroom for training all manner of entries into the Royal Navy, including the national service entry of would-be Fleet Air Arm fighter pilots.

For the next six months we sweated through courses on seamanship, anti-submarine warfare, communications, navigation, parade training and how to be a naval officer. Much of our time was spent tied up to a buoy in Portland Harbour and it was there that I was to get airborne for the first time in uniform, when we were given a single air experience flight in an RAF Sunderland. The grand old aircraft landed inside the harbour and took us on a run along the south coast at low level, circling over Calshot to let us see the three Princess flying boats on the bank there, two cocooned and one apparently in flying order.

En route to Pensacola in June 1954. Left to right, back row: Miller, Bradbury, Caine, Smith, Harvey, Hopkins, Hawes; front row: Ogilvy, Phillips, the author.

Indefat also gave us some sea time and was involved in exercises in the Atlantic and the Mediterranean, so as well as bouts of seasickness we felt as if we were getting closer to the action. During this time their lordships at the Admiralty realised they weren't going to get their money's worth out of us in the two years they had us in their power. Therefore they changed the rules and announced that if we wanted to continue with our dream of becoming Fleet Air Arm pilots we must sign on for a four-year short service commission. All twenty of us signed. I had left the comparative comfort of West House, Mirfield, where I lived with my father, Richard, a tool-maker with a Brighouse engineering firm; my mother, Nellie, the daughter of the Rastrick barber; and two sisters, Jean and Josephine.

These were the days of the Cold War and Britain was broke after her efforts in the Second World War. The Americans offered several European countries, including Britain, the Mutual Defense Assistance Program (MDAP), to boost NATO capability against the growing Soviet threat. This programme assisted with rearming and with military training. And so it was that when, in June 1954, we graduated from our upper yardman training programme as fully fledged midshipmen, ten of us were fortunate enough to be sent to do our flying training with the US Navy, starting in Pensacola, Florida. As luck would have it, the only ship that could get us to the States in time for the start of our course was an all-first-class affair, the Cunarder RMS *Media*.

On the *Media* we met six more Royal Navy officers who were travelling to the same course and who were all lieutenants who had graduated through the Naval College at Dartmouth. In the US Naval Air Station at Pensacola, the lieutenants were accommodated in the bachelor officers' quarters in comparative luxury, while we short service midshipmen messed with the American Naval Aviation cadets.

The Naval Air Station at Pensacola was, and still is, a massive organisation. It has its own deep-water harbour where carriers can get alongside, a large airfield, extensive living accommodation and university-standard lecture theatres. Within 30 miles there were several other outlying airfields and the American training system moved the students from one field to another for the various phases of basic training. We did our preflight training at Mainside, Pensacola, training to solo at Whiting Field, formation flying at Saufley Field, bombing, gun firing and deck landing from Barin, and instrument flying and night flying at Corry. The aircraft used at all these bases was the North American SNJ, or Harvard as it is known in the UK. And the size of the operation was huge. At Whiting Field alone there were more Harvards on the line than we had aircraft in the whole of the Fleet Air Arm. Where the UK was sending, on average, fifteen students into this programme every six months, the Americans were injecting thirty a week!

The preflight training at Mainside was riveting for that first four weeks before flying. The organisation picked you up into a fast-moving, highly disciplined, and very professionally run training machine. As part of the familiarisation with the SNJ our twenty-strong group was taken to an engine-running familiarisation pen. Here, in a Dutch barn arrangement, were about ten Pratt & Whitney R-1340 radial engines, which powered the trainer we were shortly to use, each mounted on a steel frame and operated from a small control panel behind a protective glass window. On this rig we were to demonstrate that we understood the start-up procedure and the means of control through the throttle and the propeller pitch lever. We stood in line waiting to be called to a vacant rig, watching impressive fires being produced by over-priming, and the whole scene produced an ear-ringing din.

The American training system was quite different from that in RAF Training Command, where those from our course who stayed back in the UK were trained. With the US Navy, each phase of training consisted of a set number of flights, each of which was pre-planned to the nth degree and with a printed form for each sortie (see opposite).

Each sortie lasted on average one hour twenty minutes and no matter how much experience a student had or how well he was progressing, he would be put through every facet of the sortie as written up. We learned from our fellow students being trained by the RAF that if they were learning fast, they would move through the syllabus at a higher rate and would go solo earlier. Here in Pensacola, you didn't solo until you had done the requisite nineteen trips.

The SNJ aircraft was a great trainer. We each had to pass a blindfold cockpit check before our first instructional flight, to demonstrate familiarity with the position of switches and controls. I remember my first sortie, watching the stick and various controls being moved by the instructor in the back seat and the instrumentation that we had been studying in books, finally moving, and I had that uneasy feeling that this was all going to be too difficult. By flight three I was keen as mustard. It was, I suppose, a fairly complicated aircraft for an initial trainer, with propeller pitch control and retractable landing gear from the beginning, but it demonstrated well all the features needed in basic flying training (see colour plate 1).

One of the American cadets had been a top-dressing pilot before joining the programme. He became the talk of the town one day when, with his instructor

A typical flight report during pre-solo training.

| CNATRA Form **ATJ-13-1** (REV. 4-54) PAT | | BINDER MARGIN DO NOT WRITE ABOVE THIS LINE | | | Navy—PPO CNATRA, Pensacola, Fla. |

Only maneuvers which have been introduced prior to or on this flight in accordance with the syllabus shall be graded. Attributes will be graded on every flight. Marks shall be awarded comparatively on the basis of the expected progress toward the established standard.

MANEUVER	Unsat.	Below Average	Average	Above Average	COMMENTS
Cockpit Check			✓		
Level Flight			✓		(Check one) Instructional Flight ✓ Check Flight ☐
Turns			✓		
Taxiing			✓		(Check one)
Take-Off		✓			Up ✓ Down ☐
Slow Flight			✓		
Transitions			✓		take off — from
Landing Pattern			✓		Touch +go landings.
Stalls			✓		always swerves.
Spirals			✓		Either direction +
Landing					both directions
Spin					
Emergencies			✓		
Approaches			✓		
X-Wind Landing Procedure					
Headwork			✓		
Reaction Toward Flt.				✓	
Air Discipline			✓		
Mental Attitude				✓	
Total Marks this hop		1	13	2	
Cumulative Flt. Totals		5	58	16	

SATISFACTORY

M.D.

Student EAGLES, J.D.   Original Class   Type Plane SNJ   Flight No. A7

Date 9/3/54   Training Unit BTU-15

Instructor's Signature

BASIC PRIMARY PRE-SOLO

in the back seat, he had an engine failure on the climb out after take-off and he immediately rolled inverted and pulled through, back to the runway! They made it but the word was that his instructor couldn't speak for days.

The social life during the course was as riveting as the flying and the American government paid us all a small cheque monthly to bring our pay up to the same level as the American cadets. On the weekend after 'cheque day' we would cash them in at the cash desk of the San Carlos Hotel in downtown Pensacola and often take one large room there for five or six of us to bed down in if the night's activities were extended. On one such night, at about three in the morning, the door of the room burst open and in came the hotel detective and a couple of uniformed policemen. 'OK,' said one of the cops. 'Which of you guys is Horatio Nelson?' We had all signed in with the usual 'Mickey Mouse' or 'Winston Churchill' signatures, and Nelson's signature was the nearest to the registration number of our car, which was parked facing the wrong way on a one-way street!

Another indication of the quality of the training programme was the Americans' approach to crosswind landing training. There was a dedicated airfield in the area for this subject, Choctaw, which had six runways arranged as a hexagon so that you could select the crosswind angle you required from whatever direction there was wind.

After the pre-solo and aerobatics phase we moved to Saufley Field, where we flew formation training sorties for a month – twenty-three sorties. We were arranged in flights of six, plus one instructor with nerves of steel. We graduated from two to four and finally six-plane exercises. At Saufley we had to do spells of duty out on the airfield controlling taxiing traffic at a taxiway intersection, and to deal with the calls of nature the base had placed an outside loo alongside the taxiway. Inevitably, a taxiing aircraft left the taxiway one day and clipped the said convenience with its wing tip. The subsequent aircraft accident report, under 'Remarks of the Administrative Authority', read, 'When ya gotta go, ya gotta go.'

Our move to Barin Field in January 1955 put us into the SNJ-5, which had a deck hook, and here we had the unforgettable experience of training for deck landing. We had fifteen flights of 'field carrier landing practice' on a satellite airfield, with our instructor at the runway touchdown point signalling with 'bats'. My progress in this phase was slow – I was always uncomfortable with getting so slow on the approach. The normal approach speed for the SNJ was 80 knots, slowing to 75 knots on finals. Here we were approaching at 70 knots and hanging on the prop on the finals turn. When the batsman gave the 'cut' signal, the instruction was to chop to idle power and simultaneously hit full forward stick, quickly followed by full back stick as the aircraft dropped to the deck. The debrief from the instructor after my final field practice trip made it fairly clear that he didn't expect me to make the grade on the trip to the ship the following day, but the whole exercise went like clockwork and I did my six deck landings without a waved off approach; '6 for 6' – a point of huge pride. I was so adrenaline-fired by the experience that after my sixth landing a crewman had to jump up on the wing and remind me that that was my lot. Time to get out and let the next guy in! The ship was the USS *Monterey*, a Second World War wooden-decked, small escort carrier that the US Navy now used only as a training ship (see colour plates 2 and 3).

Formation training at Saufley Field, Pensacola, in November 1954.

Also at Barin Field, we had our first taste of air-to-air gunnery against a towed banner target. The SNJ-6 had a 0.5in Browning machine gun installed externally along the engine cowling, with the breech protruding into the cockpit and firing through the propeller arc through an interrupter gear. We had to 'hand charge' the gun (i.e. cock it) by pulling back on a simple handle on the breech as we turned in for the first live run, and the noise and smell of cordite when the trigger was pulled was stirring stuff. The gunsight was a simple fixed cross but the whole arrangement worked well and I ended up with a respectable score. Later, in Venoms and Hunters back in the UK, air-to-air gun firing was to be my favourite occupation.

There were two or three aircraft on the line (out of thirty or forty equipped with guns) that had suffered a malfunctioning interrupter gear and had achieved a neat ½in hole through one propeller blade. Where this hole had been safely central to the blade, the other blade was drilled out to balance it, and you could tell from the ground when one of these was in the circuit, the usual unmistakable whine of the Pratt & Whitney R-1340 having an additional whistle.

Bombing, also in the SNJ-6, was a different story for me. We had to track the target from a 30-degree dive, pull out of the dive at a given height and 'pickle off' the bomb three seconds after starting the pull-out. My US marine instructor, who circled the target at the pull-out height to confirm that we obeyed the minimum height rules, wrote, 'This student may be a gunner but he's no bomber.' The weapons and deck-landing phase was completed in thirty flights over two months and was the most satisfying period in the whole programme. We found that the basics of flying the SNJ were now becoming second nature, and we were now able to superimpose new skills on top.

A memory of the Barin phase is of stopping at an isolated bar on the way back to the camp one Sunday night after a day at the beach; it was a well-known, scruffy, one-storey watering hole. Among those sitting at the bar was a customer who had clearly had more booze than was good for him and he was in a violent argument with the barman/owner, who had obviously just refused to serve him any more. The barman turned his attention to us new arrivals as the drunk stormed out. A few minutes later there was an enormous crash as a large truck drove in through the wall behind us, reversed, revved up and roared off down the highway we had just negotiated. Piqued, apparently, at the unsympathetic service.

For the final phase of basic training, and still on the SNJ, we moved on to Correy Field for the basic instruments phase and night flying. The instrument flying exercises, carried out 'under the hood' (a canvas cover that cut out all external view), called for a lot of deep concentration and heartfelt muttering – the other end of the spectrum from weaponry. We had four or five set patterns to learn to perform, controlling simultaneously speed, height and heading changes to tight limits. An example is shown below.

The sorties here lasted for two and a half hours on average and were flown from the back seat with no outside visibility. Very dehydrating. Then, finally, night flying, a new adrenaline-charged sport. I remember doing my one and only wheels-up approach on this exercise, thankfully realising it before round out and calling 'overshooting' before being spotted by the runway lookout. It is good to get a fright like that at an early stage to kill the inevitable growing overconfidence. No one had spotted it and I didn't say a word!

That was the end of our basic training phase and it was completed in 190 flying hours – much longer than the students in the UK were being given and I guess pretty luxurious by today's measure, too. An indication of the difference between the US Navy and the RAF programmes was that only one of our number out of the ten in the USA failed the course and back in the UK they lost four of their ten. I have often wondered if I would have made it with the RAF's expectation of a higher progress rate.

Now we had 'advanced' to enjoy. The American system graded the students coming out of basic training as jet fighter material or 'other'. The 'other' could lead to the advanced training phase being in multi-engined

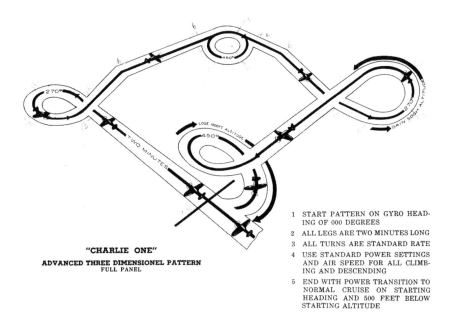

"CHARLIE ONE"
ADVANCED THREE DIMENSIONEL PATTERN
FULL PANEL

1 START PATTERN ON GYRO HEAD-
   ING OF 000 DEGREES
2 ALL LEGS ARE TWO MINUTES LONG
3 ALL TURNS ARE STANDARD RATE
4 USE STANDARD POWER SETTINGS
   AND AIR SPEED FOR ALL CLIMB-
   ING AND DESCENDING
5 END WITH POWER TRANSITION TO
   NORMAL CRUISE ON STARTING
   HEADING AND 500 FEET BELOW
   STARTING ALTITUDE

An instrument training pattern.

aircraft, namely the SNB, a Beech 18 derivative known to the RAF as the Expeditor. Alternatively, students could be bled off to helicopter training at the same point. All the British students were sent to jet fighter training, presumably at the request of the Admiralty. This training, carried out in Texas at Naval Air Stations at Corpus Christie and at Kingsville, involved exercises in three different aircraft types: the North American T-28C Trojan, the Lockheed TV-2 (a naval trainer version of the F-80), and finally the Grumman F9F-2 Panther.

It was now May 1955 and we had been with the US Navy for ten months. Our group of sixteen Brits from the RMS *Media* had spread out through the programme and I joined the T-28 programme at Kingsville with several American friends and two others from the UK. There were two interconnecting airfields at Kingsville, one being used for the piston-engined T-28 and the other for jets (see colour plate 4).

The T-28 was a most comfortable and well-equipped aircraft and it had the luxury of a nose wheel so that, unlike with the SNJ, you could see straight ahead on the ground so there was no more need to do 'clearing turns' while taxiing. And it was powerful, with its throaty Wright Cyclone engine. I see from my notes at the time I was impressed that it 'continued to accelerate easily during the climb out'! It was fitted with a dive brake, which allowed jet-style penetration and approach techniques, and it was also extremely well equipped with avionics. It had radio gear for MDF (manual direction finding), ADF (automatic direction finding), VOR (VHF omni-range), ILS (instrument landing system) and had both VHF and UHF radio. Back at home six months later, I was to find that our most up-to-date front-line fighter, the Sea Hawk, boasted only VHF radio and TACAN, a decidedly inferior fit. And, again, here at Kingsville the scale of the training operation was mind-boggling. There were seemingly acres of T-28s parked over an enormous dispersal area. After briefing for your flight you would find your assigned aircraft number and catch a 'bus' – a tractor-drawn stand-on trailer – which would plough up and down the aircraft lines until you found your mount (see colour plate 5).

We started the Kingsville training by being put through the bail-out trainer. This was an old Grumman F6F Hellcat piston-engined fighter set up in a static rig that maintained it in a tail up (i.e. level) attitude. One by one we strapped into it and closed the canopy and an engineer started and ran up the engine to full power from engine-control equipment mounted externally. An instructor shook an aileron to signal 'bail out' and we went through the procedure of unstrapping, opening the canopy and leaping out into the slipstream of the mighty Pratt & Whitney Double Wasp engine, running at full chat. There was a large thoughtfully placed net stretched between wing trailing edge and tail to catch you and you had to be in the net within some set time recorded on the instructor's stopwatch if you were to avoid going through the whole hair-raising procedure again. But we looked enviously at the Hellcat and wished we could enjoy meeting it in proper circumstances (see colour plate 6).

The first training phase at Kingsville was in the 'all-weather flight', being lectured at in the mornings and flying in the back seat of the T-28, 'under the hood', in the afternoons. There were similar basic instrument patterns to those we flew at Corry in the SNJ, but here we moved on to gaining a full instrument rating using all the T-28's radio gear. We were back to three-hour trips of intense concentration on the gauges, on some occasions two in one day. It was a huge relief to get through the instruments phase and start to fly the T-28 in the tactics phase from the front seat. We had a flight of five students (four Americans and myself), a lieutenant US Navy instructor, and twenty-two flights of pure joy to get through. We were introduced to fighter tactics and, bearing in mind that the average age of us students was 19 (I was the youngest), I felt the instructor had his time cut out trying to keep the whole exercise safe. After a brush-up on formation and aerobatics, we spent much of the time scrapping in one-on-one fighter manoeuvring and we were rewarded with a memorable formation land away to Dallas for a weekend. Could life get any better than this? (See colour plate 7.)

Life did get even better, though a little more serious, when we moved over to the jet field and did our jet familiarisation in the TV-2. We flew twelve trips in this jet trainer, all dual, and it was a little sobering to find the very noticeable degree of unresponsiveness in engine control that this old but much revered jet had compared with the pistons, and the high degree of anticipation needed when making power corrections on the approach to land (see colour plate 8).

Approach speeds were higher, of course (from memory about 105 knots), and flatter approaches were required so the engine could be kept at a higher and so more responsive power setting. But the performance was impressive. On my first familiarisation trip we reached 48,000ft altitude and I didn't get higher than that for several years in my flying career. The air-conditioning system was even more impressive! We could produce snow from the cabin cooling system on take-off, and in Kingsville, Texas, in July that seemed pretty clever. The TV-2 was, of course, developed from the original P-80 Shooting Star, the first American operational jet fighter back in early 1945. It was interesting to compare it later with the de Havilland Vampire, developed in the UK at about the same time and which we were about to encounter as a trainer when we got home. The Vampire trainer had a side-by-side seating arrangement that was partly responsible for its uglier cockpit layout. And, unlike the TV-2, it also had pretty uncomfortable behaviour when recovering from a dive to limiting Mach number using air brakes. An oscillation reaching plus and minus 3g was possible. The TV-2 was not so lively in these conditions but it was perhaps not so manoeuvrable in the normal flight envelope either. We didn't solo the TV-2 and so couldn't 'mess around' in it as we could the Vampire. What *was* impressive with the TV-2, and indeed with all the American aircraft I encountered, was the normal fuel load and so the range or endurance. All our sorties in it and in our final aircraft type, the F9F Panther, were of around one-and-a-half hours' duration, compared with the UK's Sea Hawk and Vampire typical endurance (soon to be encountered) of one hour, or one hour and ten minutes at the most.

After twelve sorties in the TV-2 we finally flew our first single-seat fighter, the F9F-2 Panther. This was the US Navy's most extensively used fighter in the recent Korean War, with more than 1,000 built. It was fitted with wing-tip tanks, 4 × 20mm cannon and the engine was a Pratt & Whitney J42-P-8 – actually a Rolls-Royce Nene scaled up to 1⅛ size (see colour plate 9).

Three of us from the UK were ready at the same time for this final phase and, since the instruction was organised in flights of three, we arranged for an all-RN flight, to be called Limey Flight. Lt A.M.G. (thought to stand for All Mighty God) Pearson,★ Midshipman John Gingell (later a captain with Aer Lingus), and myself were assigned a US marine instructor, Capt. Newmark, who was an archetypal US marine. After one sortie of type familiarisation, which was closely chased by an instructor, we began the final phase of tactics, formation and then gunnery against a towed banner target.

On one of our four ship formation take-offs, Capt. Newmark briefed us and then gave us a particular instruction concerning the pre-take-off actions. The main runway ran close and parallel to a public road and there was a run up area between the runway and the road where aircraft stopped to make final checks before take-off. At the fence, which separated the run up area from the road, was a viewing spot where passers-by could watch the camp's operations. We were, he said, to line up tidily at the run-up area with tailpipes to the fence, and adjust the aircraft's heading 'until you have in your rear view mirror the maximum number of "ceevillians" (he spat this word out as though it was poison) and then you turn up (run up the engine) and blow them away.'

The F9 had fairly light control forces, which made for very nice handling. The roll rate was exceptional – I believe 360 degrees a second at around 10,000ft at 300 knots. Full aileron would knock your head against the canopy side. Having a more modern engine control system than the TV-2, the engine response was a clear improvement over that aircraft and so it removed to some extent the bogey of jets needing much engine anticipation on the approach. It must have been a very pleasant aircraft to take to the deck, though we weren't given that pleasure. Certainly it gave a lot of confidence in the air-to-air gun-firing pattern and I was able to come away with an 8 per cent hit score, which was a good one among the students.

★ We also had a Lt C.A.M. Comins; the initials were thought to stand for Christ All Mighty.

During my time in the States, although not a natural letter-writer, I kept up a series of progress reports to Dad, who was at this time a tool-maker with a cotton-industry machinery manufacturer in Brighouse, Yorkshire. He was always keen to hear about the mechanics of flying – especially the engines involved – and I was always proud to tell him of my progress. Many years later, after his death, I found he had kept all these scrawled notes in a series of tobacco tins and they have helped me recall some of my early navy time.

We came home from the USA in dribs and drabs, as each individual completed the course. Lt Tony Pearson and I were the first home, sailing from New York on 31 August 1955 on the RMS *Queen Elizabeth*, and I was met by my mother and sister, Jeanie, at Southampton. I enjoyed four weeks' leave at West House, Mirfield, and it was during that time that I began to take a much stronger interest in beekeeping – my father's main hobby. He kept around twelve stocks of bees in hives behind the house and sold 200–300lb of honey each year. He combined strong interests in nature – what flowers and trees were in blossom and giving nectar – with his professional engineering, building 3½in-gauge steam locomotives in his well-equipped workshop. I have always regretted not spending much more time with him.

After leave, I was brought back to the reality of navy life with various short, non-flying courses. The first was the divisional officers' course at HMS *Victory* in Portsmouth. Parade training, including sword drill, was now in the uniform of an acting temporary probationary sub lieutenant. We were messed in the shore station just outside the Portsmouth Dockyard gates and I remember the intimidating wardroom dining room with a fabulous mural of the Battle of Trafalgar and a wardroom steward behind every chair. A far cry from the pressed-steel plate/trays we had queued up with for our meals at Kingsville just three months earlier!

In November most of our original course slowly reassembled at the Naval Air Station at Ford, near Littlehampton (later an open prison), and we were introduced to British aircraft, namely the Vampire and Sea Hawk, and to British procedures. Inevitably there was some disappointment at finding the facilities, and particularly the availability of aircraft, markedly inferior to standards in the States. We quickly got the word that to compare the two openly, or worse, to complain, marked you down for heat from the stalwarts for whom this scene was normal. But it also became clear that the degree of individual initiative that the Royal Navy allowed its officers was far greater than we had noted in the USN, even recognising that we had been in a training regime there.

Operating from Ford, the first big difference was inevitably the weather! Although my logbook showed that I had been through nearly sixty hours of instrument flying with the USN, I had less than one hour in actual instrument conditions; all the rest was under the hood. At Ford, after getting familiarised with the Vampire, we were often in clag for more than half the flying time. I remember one early solo Vampire trip when I staggered up to 42,000ft in cloud, turned around and started my procedure to get back to base, never having seen the natural horizon! But, of course, it was by now November. The other big difference was the aircraft. With memories of the Panther still alive, the two-seat Vampire, which was our first introduction to Fleet Air Arm flying, seemed a definite step down. It had no avionics other than a VHF radio and our Ford aircraft had no weapons capability. (In fact the Vampire was a very capable and forgiving trainer and gave good service for many more years.) (See colour plate 10.)

Our Squadron at Ford, 764 Squadron, was effectively a holding unit for pilots waiting for assignment to either further training units or to front-line squadrons. We were to be held there until mid-February 1956, when we were to start our operational conversion course on the Hawker Sea Hawk aircraft at Lossiemouth in Scotland. Our squadron had a mix of Vampire, Sea Hawk and Wyvern aircraft and the pilot population varied during those weeks from too many to *far* too many for its small complement of aircraft. When our course from the States began to reassemble the shortage of aircraft was so acute that the CO introduced a watch system; half of us to be available for the mornings only and the other half for the afternoons. On our half days 'off' we would visit other squadrons at Ford, seeking a ride in anything getting airborne with a spare seat. I got some flying time in a Dragonfly helicopter and, later, in the rear seat of a Fairey Firefly, never suspecting that I would be seeing more of this Second World War piston-engined aircraft the following year. But eventually we managed to get our hands on 764's Sea Hawk aircraft and life took on a happier hue.

The Sea Hawk was the Royal Navy's front-line fighter and was operational at that time in four or five aircraft carriers in various parts of the world. It was a delightful aircraft to fly, with power-assisted ailerons, the Rolls-Royce Nene engine giving 5,000lb thrust, and it was a single-seater! Here at Ford we used it to practise formation flying, low-level navigation and, of course, aerobatics whenever possible. Weaponry training was to come at the Operational Conversion Unit (OCU) at Lossiemouth (see colour plate 11).

A frequent sortie out of Ford was a map-reading reconnaissance exercise. We were given a sealed envelope to be opened in the air and we then had to work out a course to reach a given latitude and longitude and note what was at that location.

Towards the end of February 1956, ten of us started the OCU course at the Naval Air Fighter School at the Royal Naval Air Station at Lossiemouth, HMS Fulmar. The staff there were somewhat contemptuous of USN trained pilots. The feeling was that the American programme was so much by numbers that over there they could train a monkey to fly. One of our number was failed, having battled his way through the US programme and achieved 'Wings'. But the rest of us hung on through twenty-five hours' flying time in the Vampire, doing largely instrument flying training, before finally getting to the Sea Hawk and the more interesting tactics, formation and camera-gunnery phase. We graduated as fully fledged RN fighter pilots and duly reported back to the air station at Ford again to await appointment to a front-line squadron and hopefully some ship time.

During the early 1950s the Royal Navy had developed three significant improvements to the operation of aircraft from carriers. They were the angled deck, the mirror landing device and the steam catapult. The angled deck introduced a skewing of the centre line of the aircraft's landing area to port that allowed the landing aircraft a clear run ahead, back into the air, if it failed to pick up an arrester wire. Previously, if an aircraft hook failed to pick up a wire, there was the likelihood of the offending aircraft continuing up the deck and running into the deck park of previously landed aircraft. To avoid this, a steel wire barrier was raised at the end of the expected landing run, to contain any 'bolter', i.e. an aircraft that missed the wires. Although this would protect the aircraft parked up forward, the barrier made a mess of the aircraft running into it. The angled deck reduced deck accidents significantly. The idea was first put forward by Capt. D.R.F. Cambell, DSC, RN in 1951, although it was the Americans who first modified a ship to this standard. The RN initially merely 'painted on' an angled centre line and realigned the arrester wires, until HMS *Hermes* was commissioned in 1959 with the full angle and deck extension.

Next, the mirror landing sight was introduced to replace the batsman, who previously gave landing pilots signals using high visibility 'bats' to help with line-up, approach angle and engine cut point. The device was one large mirror, concave about a vertical axis, facing aft, mounted on the port side of the deck and gyro-stabilised against pitching movements of the ship. Aft of the mirror a source-light shone forward into it and was reflected back up the approach path at the required approach angle of around 3 degrees. On each side of the mirror was a horizontal row of datum lights and the approaching pilot controlled his position above and below the ideal approach path by keeping the 'meatball' (the reflection of the source light) in line with the horizontal datum lights. If he was high, the meatball would appear higher than the datums, and vice versa. The mirror (now the 'landing sight') has been much modified since those days but the principles remain the same (see colour plate 12).

And finally there was the steam catapult. Catapult machinery in carriers in the early 1950s was powered by hydro-pneumatics and gave a 'peaky' acceleration. The steam catapult, developed by Brown Bros of Edinburgh, has proved capable of greater power and a smoother ride using this smaller and simpler piece of machinery. (Today, though, the US Navy is introducing EMALS – an electromechanical aircraft launch system that uses an electromagnetic accelerator motor.)

These three innovations, largely the first two, gave a step improvement in the safety of deck operations and so reduced the loss rate of pilots. I assume that this was partly the reason that in 1956, the Admiralty found they were training more pilots than they needed in the squadrons and so reduced training rates for a while. In an effort to reduce the number of pilots waiting for 'slots' in front-line squadrons, a request was put out at our Ford holding squadron for volunteers to serve for two years on loan to the Royal Australian Navy's Fleet Air Arm, which was short of pilots. The expectation was that volunteers would join the RAN's newly acquired aircraft carrier, HMAS *Melbourne*, hopefully in its night fighter squadron equipped with the de Havilland Sea Venom. I saw this as a route to an embarked squadron earlier than looked likely in the UK, as well as a view of another part of the world, and was the first of our course to take up the offer.

2

Australia

On 26 June I sailed in the Orient Line ship RMS *Orontes* to Sydney via Gibraltar, Naples, Suez, Aden, Colombo, Freemantle, Adelaide and Melbourne; a freebie holiday in itself! In Freemantle I visited the Australian Navy office to pick up my orders and I found to my horror that, rather than Sea Venoms, I was appointed to 851 Squadron, a shore-based Firefly squadron, training observers. To say that I was disappointed would be falling well short of the truth. The Firefly was an ex-Second World War piston-engined aircraft that had been the mainstay of the Fleet Air Arm's anti-submarine and strike roles since that conflict, but which was nearing the end of its service life. On 2 August I arrived at the Royal Australian Naval Air Station (RANAS) Nowra, about 100 miles south of Sydney and close to some fabulous beaches on Australia's south-east coast. After sorting out my gear and settling in I asked to see the captain to explain that I had just completed jet training and that Australia House in London had led us to expect that volunteers from the UK would be used in their jet squadrons. The captain very quickly made it clear that I would be taking up whatever job I was given and showed me the door. And so I and two other volunteers, Arthur Arundel and Ian Ogilvy, who followed me out about three weeks later, formed what we called 'The First Piston Reversion Course' and learned to fly this venerable beast.

In fact, experience on the Firefly was invaluable and we were very fortunate to have it. Every different type flown adds something to a pilot's experience and instincts. The Firefly was somewhat heavy on the controls and, of course, not nearly as responsive in pitch or roll as the jet fighters we had just left (see colour plate 13). But it was very stable, easy to trim out, and the Rolls-Royce Griffon engine was highly reliable. In fact, there was no engine failure on the Firefly during my two years there, although one of our number (who was known as Rough-Running Rogers) tended to find

The author, Arundel and Ogilvy on the 'First Piston Reversion Course' at RANAS Nowra in 1956.

that many of the aircraft he was assigned would sound suspect as soon as he coasted out over the Tasman Sea and he would return to have it checked.

The flying environment at Nowra was very different to the States and to the UK in that there was little or no other air traffic in the area and the scenery was wall-to-wall outback bush. My first briefing on the local area was along the lines of, 'The airfield is a bit hard to pick out visually from the air – just look for a hill shaped like a woman's breast and you've got it!' (Nowra Hill was indeed alongside the field.) Discipline was somewhat more relaxed than in the UK, but the general efficiency and keenness on the task were every bit as good and the Australian sense of humour was a real treat. I remember asking one of the Fury squadron pilots why we Brits were usually referred to as Kippers. The snappy answer was, 'Cos you're all two-faced, yellow, gutless bastards!'

Our task in 851 Squadron was to train observers; the back-seater who in an air force would be called the navigator. A typical training sortie might be over-sea navigation with wind-finding. We would coast out from a recognisable point and head off until out of sight of land. Then set up a wind-finding exercise; dropping a smoke float into the sea and flying a pattern around it that would bring you back over the smoke float if there was no wind, and estimating the wind strength and direction when the set pattern did not bring you back directly over it. The observer would then calculate the heading to steer to get us back over the coast-out point and we would note the degree of navigational error on coasting in. Fortunately for the soul, this type of exercise was interspersed with more interesting overland navigation exercises and some bombing and rocketing practice.

On 27 November 1956, a flight of four of us had just finished a wind-finding exercise out over the south coast and were rejoining the formation to return to Nowra. As we formed up, one of the four flew through the form-up pattern head on, collided with my aircraft and removed 5ft of my starboard wing,★ including the aileron. We were over Jervis Bay at the time, about 10 miles from Nowra airfield, and I broadcast a Mayday call and tried to get the aircraft under control. With full power and full left stick and rudder, I could only keep wings level at 165 knots and above. At this speed I was losing height and I realised I was going to have to ditch in the sea. The sea state in the bay was pretty smooth and so I turned on the radio altimeter to help judge height above the sea for the final round out. The aircraft rolled right slightly just before impact but stayed on the surface throughout and we clambered out. The other aircraft in the collision had been flown by one of our group of three Brits, Sub Lt Arthur Arundel. He wasn't so lucky, his aircraft crashing into the bay half a mile from our ditching, with the loss of both crew. My observer, Sub Lt Debus, and I were both fished out by helicopter and two days later I was put back into the air, as was the tradition after such experiences.

Arthur Arundel had been a good friend. At the board of inquiry it transpired that he had been up half the night on watch duty and had asked to be excused from that sortie since he was tired. But apparently he had been persuaded to do it, since we had no other aircrew. Arthur came from Hull and we had pulled his leg during a recent shipping tragedy when, after a sinking, the headlines of the *Sydney Telegraph* announced, 'Three men trapped alive inside hull.' I went to see his parents when I got back to the UK later to explain the accident, although I didn't mention the tiredness aspect.

At New Year in 1957, Sub Lt Ian Ogilvy and myself, the two remaining British pilots on loan, were given a change to 805 Squadron flying the Hawker Sea Fury. This squadron, too, was shore-based and would not deploy on to a carrier, but to move on to the Fury was a huge treat. The squadron occupied itself with practising weapons delivery and tactics, and there was even talk of starting an aerobatic team. I had already managed to get an

★ In February 2016, Greg Stubbs, a diver from Nowra, exercising at the Firefly wreck, measured the missing portion at 7ft 3in!

occasional trip in the Fury, courtesy of a magnanimous squadron CO and a lot of pleading. The aircraft was a development of the Hawker Tempest, which had served with the RAF from April 1944, but the Sea Fury did not see service until 1948. It was designed as a single-seat fighter/bomber, with a Bristol Centaurus eighteen-cylinder sleeve-valve, radial (air-cooled) engine, in two banks of nine cylinders, a huge five-bladed propeller and a single stage, two-speed supercharger. It was cleared to 425 knots (490mph) and had a system of propeller pitch control whereby, once airborne, the pilot could pull back the pitch lever to an 'auto' position where the rpm were controlled automatically by the position of the throttle lever (see colour plate 14).

This meant that you always had the minimum rpm permitted for whatever engine boost setting you chose and so you could not inadvertently 'over-boost' the engine. The auto position could not be used in close formation, since that gave an imprecise response, but it gave jet-engine-like single-lever engine control for other activities. Flying control forces were low except when diving at high altitude, when Mach effects stiffened them up. At low-level, roll response was good up to the limiting speeds, assisted by spring tab ailerons.

Earlier in the Sea Fury's life, engine reliability had been a weak area. Being a sleeve valve design, oil pressure was a must and loss of oil meant your time in the air was extremely limited. This was in contrast to the Rolls-Royce Griffon in the Firefly, which would keep running sometimes for ten minutes after the oil was gone. But by 1956 the Centaurus had been made much more reliable and was by now no problem. I had only one engine failure in my eighteen months on the aircraft, and that ended happily by putting it down on a disused airfield at Jervis Bay.

Nowra was the permanent home to four squadrons: 851 with Fireflys; 805 with Sea Furys; 724 Training squadron, which had Vampires, Sea Furys and Firefly Trainers; and finally Station Flight, with Dakotas and Dragonfly helicopters. In addition, 808 Squadron, with Sea Venoms, and 824 Squadron, with Fairey Gannets, were based at Nowra when not embarked in HMAS *Melbourne* and 'parked' with 724 Squadron.

Although formally a member of 805 Squadron, in August 1957 I took on the additional task of maintenance test pilot for the station. A shortage of maintenance ratings at Nowra had led to the airfield changing to a centralised maintenance system. Instead of each squadron doing its own maintenance with its own ratings, all were put into a pool and all squadrons sent their aircraft to a central hangar for servicing and maintenance. Although unqualified, I answered a call for a volunteer to do what test flying might be

Fairey Gannets, Vampire T.22 and Sea Venom of 724 Squadron at RANAS Nowra in 1956.

needed after servicing or maintenance by this organisation. I did not fly the Dakota or the helicopter but I was current on the Firefly, Fury and Vampire. This opened up the opportunity for much more flying and started my interest in aircraft beyond their strictly military use. I began to discuss some aspects of testing with the air station's air engineer officer, Cdr John Lovell, and as time went on I studied the qualifications needed to apply for a place at the Empire Test Pilots' School (ETPS) at Farnborough.

As well as doing the test flying after engine changes, I began to take an interest in the engine maintenance itself and became involved in some of the more interesting evolutions. On one occasion, I joined the team carrying out an engine change on a Firefly and when it was completed, suggested to the chief artificer in charge that he might like to come with me on the test flight. Chief Aircraft Artificer Gover, a stern disciplinarian, was somewhat reluctant but eventually accepted. The word got around his junior ratings that he was going on the flight and I had several of them come to me the evening before suggesting I might give him 'a rough one'. I would never inflict unwanted manoeuvring on anyone, but after the long data-gathering climb was over I overflew the small village where Chief Gover lived and as we returned to the field I asked him if he would like me to do a gentle roll. Although we had been in intercom contact earlier, he didn't reply. I asked again and there was still no reply so I told him I would do a very gentle barrel roll to show that aerobatics can be enjoyable. After the roll there was still no communication so I carried on back to base. At the hangar, all hands were 'fell in' and a highly decorated platform and stepladder were in position to meet us.

After shutting down, Chief Gover got out, to be welcomed with a noisy award ceremony at the foot of the ladder, where he received an impressive medal and gaudy ribbon. He had not appreciated the demonstrated roll and it was several minutes before he would come back to be photographed with his medal! (See colour plate 15.)

Later that year, a new senior pilot joined 805 Squadron, Lt Cdr Brian Stock, also on loan from the UK. He began to work up a formation aerobatic team, leading a 'vic' of three, the other two being Sub Lt 'Blue' Davidson and myself. There was a rumour that some years before, the RAN had produced a four-aircraft Sea Fury team, but on one occasion the box man★ had overrun the leader and chopped his tail off, and so future teams were to be limited to three, with no box man (see colour plate 16).

I remember a complicated and ambitious air-show routine that, as well as formation aerobatics, included splitting up for individual aerobatic manoeuvres including simultaneous, separated, stall turns. We visited various air shows in New South Wales and Victoria with this team, including visits well out west to Mildura and Broken Hill. The scenery en route to these remote places was spectacularly empty and our navigation maps showed rivers that did not exist. For these displays, the navy indulged in a repaint of four of the team aircraft, with a gaudy silver-and-red scheme, which fortunately was not visible from inside the cockpit.

During the summer weekends another RN loan officer, Peter Henshaw, and myself frequently took the air station water bowser, a small road tanker that could transport 500 gallons of water, to one of the small settlements at Jervis Bay where several of our married squadron friends lived. They relied on rainwater from the roof for their needs and this frequently did not materialise. The air station, though, pumped water up from the nearby Shoalhaven River and so it was always plentiful. On several occasions as we made these journeys we came across bush fires being fought along the road and we would donate our load to the firefighters.

My other spare-time activity at Nowra was gliding. The air station hosted a gliding club that owned a Slingsby T.31 training glider and operated

★ The rear man of a box formation of four.

Slingsby Trainer and Nymph sailplane at the Nowra Gliding Club in 1957. The author is on the front row, fourth from the left.

on weekends. The glider was launched using a 3-ton truck borrowed from the MT section to tow-launch using 2,000ft of piano wire. After a couple of months I became the club's instructor and we taught several naval ratings to fly.

With subscriptions and naval funding help we bought an Australian-designed Schneider Nymph single-seater sailplane and later a two-seat Schneider trainer that we used to set up a two-week residential training course for the Australian Naval College. I remember giving the station commander an introductory ride in this two-seater one Sunday morning just after church. He was still in his full white uniform. I got slow on the top of a loop and some overnight rain that had found its way beneath the cockpit duckboard floor came down on to us and took the crease off his immaculate trousers.

Initially, I was homesick in Australia. The disappointment of my first appointment didn't help and neither did the news from the UK that all my recent course mates had been assigned quickly to Sea Hawk squadrons and were aboard carriers fighting the Suez War. With the foolishness of youth I envied them. But it didn't last long and I look back on that time with the Australian Fleet Air Arm as great experience. Capt.V.A.T. Smith RAN (later ADM Sir Victor Smith), the captain at Nowra, invited me to transfer to the Australian Navy but I had my eye on the new naval aircraft then coming into service in Britain, the Scimitar and the Sea Vixen.

3

The Cold War

In June 1958 I returned to the Fleet Air Arm in the UK. My journey out to Australia had been with the Orient Line through the Suez Canal and for the return I requested a route via New Zealand and through the Panama Canal. I sailed from Sydney on the *Wanganella* to Wellington and after a week's sightseeing through the North Island I joined the New Zealand Shipping Company liner *Rangitoto* for the trip back to England. It was on this cruise that I met up with a whole bunch of Kiwis about my age, who were travelling to England for some 'OE', or overseas experience, before settling down to their careers. Among them was Raewyn Leach, my wife to be, setting off for a teaching spell in London.

I was champing at the bit to get back to flying in the UK. Now a lieutenant with four-and-a-half years' service behind me, I still had only six deck landings in my logbook. In July I was glad to start the All Weather Fighter (AWF) Course at Royal Naval Air Station Yeovilton in Somerset, also known as HMS Heron, flying the de Havilland Sea Venom. There were five pilots on the course, including Lt Ian Ogilvy, also just back from his two years in Australia, and five observers. We formed into five crews but my own observer dropped out after a month's flying and I teamed up with a latecomer, Lt Jim McPhee. The main skill taught on the course was the ability of the crew to gain radar contact with an airborne target and to close to within 200yd of it, at night or in nil visibility, and be able to attack it with the aircraft's 20mm cannon. This required the observer to interpret his radar picture and chant out a patter of instructions to the pilot, which, when followed according to a pretty strict conversion of terminology into control inputs, would put the aircraft into that final firing position. The whole course took some 100 flying hours, more than a quarter of which were flown at night and, towards the end of the course, with lights out. In the next generation of all-weather fighter aircraft the new technologies were able to convert the radar information straight into a symbol in the head-up display that the pilot simply followed, but back in the 1950s, interceptions relied hugely on crew co-ordination and skill.

Inevitably, the camaraderie that built up during the four months of this course was spectacular and as we finished we wrote to the appropriate desk in Admiralty asking if all five crews could please be appointed to the same squadron, an unlikely possibility. However, four crews were kept together and posted to 891 AWF Squadron, to be embarked in HMS *Centaur*, due to operate in the Far East for a year. Only Jim McPhee and I were separated from the mob, joining 893 Squadron flying Sea Venoms in the carrier *Victorious*. Some months later the two carriers operated together around the UK for a couple of weeks before *Centaur* set off to the antipodes. Both ships anchored together for the last time in May 1959 in Cardigan Bay, and Jim and I went over to *Centaur* for a final course get together before we went on our separate ways. Sadly, that was the last time we saw Ian Ogilvy and Cyril Meek, as they were both killed in an accident in the Far East.

The Sea Venom was an excellent aircraft to operate off the deck. It was small, of course, with a maximum take-off weight of only 15,800lb and had

No. 5 AWF Course at RNAS Yeovilton in November 1958. Left to right: Ogilvy, Green, author, McPhee, Haughton, Maycock, Marjoribanks, McQueen, Barnes, Pinney.

an excellent and reliable engine, the de Havilland Ghost of 5,300lb thrust. It was easy to trim the aircraft quickly out in pitch on the approach and thereafter it was a very stable and yet manoeuvrable deck-lander. It was certainly a great advantage to gain deck operating experience and confidence in such a relatively simple aircraft. At the same time, HMS *Victorious* had embarked the first Supermarine Scimitar Squadron, 803, and although we were all impressed by this 30,000lb monster, those of us who were new to squadron deck operations undoubtedly grew in confidence more quickly with our more manoeuvrable Sea Venom.

Victorious was one of the happiest ships I served in. Her captain, Charles Coke, was one of nature's gentlemen and the entire ship's company loved him. Our commander (Air) was John Treacher (later ADM Sir John, commander-in-chief, Fleet), who in typical style took up his appointment as 'Wings' by flying aboard in one of our squadron Sea Venoms.

Victorious had a 775ft, fully angled (8¾ degrees) flight deck, two parallel track steam catapults, the new deck landing mirror and an air defence radar,

HMS *Victorious* makes a formal entry into harbour in 1959.

De Havilland Sea Venom FAW.22 of 893 Squadron on HMS *Victorious* in 1959.

Type 984, which was considered the best in the world at that time. During the thirteen months we were embarked in her, *Victorious* operated in the North Sea, the Atlantic and the Mediterranean, exercising with the other NATO navies and generally staying in good weaponry practice in case the Cold War should turn hot. The Scimitar squadron practised the delivery of the nuclear store we held and we in the Venom squadron worked up good accuracy using 3in rockets and 20mm cannon, firing both air-to-air against a banner target and air-to-ground strafing. But our main exercise was practising interceptions, in conjunction with the ship's 984 radar, by day and night.

Operating aircraft, a carrier normally needs to turn into wind to launch and recover them, and this usually delays the ship from making good her intended course. So the shorter the time the ship is required to stay on her 'flying course', the better. For this reason, squadrons when landing on aim to land with the shortest time interval possible between aircraft. When an aircraft, hook down, lands into the wires, it is brought to a stop and the wire then exerts a small rearward force that causes the aircraft to run backwards. The pilot allows this to occur and during this rearward movement the wire falls out of the hook. The pilot then puts on power to move the aircraft forward up the deck, out of the landing area and the wire can then be reset (i.e. trundled back down the deck into its position ready to be available for the hook of the next aircraft down). The time between the aircraft touching down and the moment when the wire it used is fully reset is the minimum interval possible between aircraft touchdowns. If an aircraft arrives over the deck before the wire is reset, he is 'waved off' and must go round again for a second landing attempt.

The interval into the wires is either controlled by the ship's radar controller, when the aircraft are being recovered individually (e.g. at night) or by the individual pilot if the aircraft returns to the ship visually. In a visual recovery case, each pilot must organise his own interval from the one ahead and this skill of controlling how far one is running behind the aircraft in front, in time terms, is a skill that must be learned with experience. At the end of our embarked time in HMS *Victorious*, 893 Squadron had got this interval down to an average of fourteen seconds, a figure of which we were proud. Towards the end of 1958, two of our aircraft were converted to carry the Firestreak air-to-air missile and, although it looked ungainly on our small aircraft, we had now entered the missile age (the Firestreak was to be the primary weapon of the Sea Vixen, the new all-weather fighter that would replace the Sea Venom).

Exercising with the US Fleet in July 1959 in the Atlantic was a sobering event. To see HMS *Victorious* (30,000 tons) alongside the USS *Forrestal* (60,000 tons) was to put our contribution to NATO into perspective, but it was pleasing to find that our operations co-ordinated well with theirs and though our aircraft were fewer in number we concluded when we mixed it with them that we were at least equal in effectiveness. Furthermore, *Victorious's* superb 984 radar gave us an edge during our exercises with them.

The CO of 893 Squadron was Lt Cdr Eric Manuel, a very experienced naval aviator with many hours in the Sea Venom. He used to put forward a theory that, when setting up the Venom for a long-range cruise at the appropriate height (i.e. around 35,000ft), it was advisable to exceed the published best-cruising speed slightly, and then 'settle back on to it', rather than simply increase up to the required speed and then hold it. He claimed that when doing the former he ended up requiring slightly less engine power in the cruise than in the other case. He used to call it 'getting onto the step'. This did not appear to be logical and after trying his method we argued many times, but without him conceding.

After some two months of operating from the deck, the new boys in the squadron were introduced to night deck operations. We were each assigned a mentor – one of the old hands – to brief us on the mysteries and ensure we were thoroughly familiar with the night routine. My mentor was Lt 'Bunny' Warren, an old hand who had originally joined the navy as a non-commissioned pilot and who was everybody's favourite raconteur. He told me there was really no difference between deck landing by night and by day 'except this', and here he used his hands to demonstrate. 'At night, when you realise you're over the deck, you do this,' (the left hand came back smartly, signifying the throttle was chopped to idle, at the same time that the right hand went forward, signifying the stick being pushed fully forward). 'Then you count to two and if nothing happens [you don't feel the deceleration of a wire snatch] you reverse it!' (His left hand going fully forward and the right one coming fully back.) But I survived and, in fact, met Bunny several years later in Venezuela, then captain of a Boeing 707 with BOAC. Fortunately his night landing at Heathrow didn't follow this technique.

In that squadron, my first embarked, were others who had trained at Pensacola too, but who had by now much more deck experience that had been achieved while I had been taking in the delights of the Sea Fury in Australia. And one great friend, sadly lost in an accident later, was Simon Idiens, an excellent aviator, sportsman and raconteur whom I was to follow into several jobs in the coming years.

While serving in 893 Squadron, when we were disembarked from *Victorious* during October 1959 we moved the whole squadron temporarily to the Naval Air Station at Brawdy in South Wales to get in some armament practice at the various firing ranges close by. We spent two weeks of bombing, rocketing, strafing and air-to-air firing there and during our stay I saw a superb example of the art of leadership. The navy rightly celebrates Nelson's victory at Trafalgar, every year on 21 October, and during our time there we attended the Trafalgar night dinner in Brawdy's wardroom. We had already become a touch unpopular in the mess due to our inevitable spirited behaviour in the evenings during this exercise. The commander, a humourless chap, had already announced that he didn't want bad behaviour at the dinner since the guest of honour was to be the Lord Lieutenant of Carmarthenshire, Sir Grismond Picton Philipps, a very senior retired army officer. We were threatened with career-limiting punishment and our CO asked for a 'bit of decorum'.

Inevitably several firecrackers were set off as the dinner progressed and on each occasion the commander sprang to his feet, glaring in the direction of the explosion. The grand finale was when a kidney-shaped plate carrying the desert, a banana split, was hurriedly passed up one arm of the tables, fizzing before exploding. The commander overreacted substantially, standing to make a long apology and explaining to the guest of honour that the perpetrators were a visiting squadron from 'some other air station', and not normal Brawdy dwellers. When we got to the speeches stage, the commander again apologised profusely to the guest before introducing him. The lord lieutenant, in a wonderful regimental uniform that included spurs and chain mail, stood up and looked around for a short time in silence. Then he started his speech by saying, 'Tonight is Trafalgar Night – and I smell gunpowder!' He was cheered to the rafters.

From 893 Squadron I left to do the Air Warfare Instructors' (AWI) course, the RN's 'Top Gun' course, starting with six weeks of weapons and weapon-aiming theory at Whale Island, Portsmouth, the home of naval gunnery since the 1800s. Whale Island was hallowed ground to the gunnery branch and was dominated by an enormous parade ground where countless gunnery officers had learned their trade and undergone their square bashing. Service discipline was intense. One afternoon, marching back to the classroom after lunch (no one merely walked at Whaley), the two of us on the course realised we were being shouted at from across this enormous parade ground. There, about a quarter of a mile away, were two petty officer gunnery instructors, standing rigidly to attention, shouting, 'Sir, we are saluting you!'

Whaley was where I first used mathematics to solve serious problems and discovered that, when used to some purpose, maths could even be interesting. For instance, the course covered the calculation of gunsight settings to take into account variables such as the aircraft's own attitude changes with airspeed and the gravity drop of the weapon being fired. These calculations were useful years later when, at British Aerospace, the Royal Saudi Air Force had a requirement for a bombing capability for its Lightning aircraft and we had to work out a sight setting from scratch since the RAF had had no such requirement. At Whaley, too, we learned to calculate the effects of the nuclear bomb carried by Fleet Air Arm aircraft, and the various techniques of delivery.

There were only two of us taking the course and my partner was Lt 'Dudge' Dudgeon, a self-styled woman-killer. The second part of the course, the eight weeks flying part, was held at the Naval Air Fighter and Strike School at the Royal Naval Air Station Lossiemouth, on the coast of the Moray Firth in Scotland. Dudge and I travelled up by train and, as we crossed London from

Waterloo to King's Cross stations, the taxi stopped at a pedestrian crossing where a swarm of nuns were crossing the road. Dudge commented, 'Do you know, I only ever had a nun once … '

The flying at Lossiemouth was in the Hawker Hunter T.8, the navy's two-seater variant of that fine aircraft, and the experience was a sort of aviation equivalent of the Whale Island gunnery school. Adrenaline-packed and very demanding, the syllabus included rocketing, bombing and 30mm-cannon firing, both air-to-ground and air-to-air against banner targets (my favourite sport). We learned low-level strike tactics with four-ship formations, where as a wingman you stayed close and low, but must hang on in there no matter how harsh the manoeuvring of the leader. There was great rivalry between students when it came to scores and inevitably there was a tendency to get close to the target. I recall being in the dive on a cannon-strafing run and seeing Dudge ahead just finishing his run. As he pulled out, the fact that his wing tip vortices touched the ground very shortly after he stopped firing showed how close he had come to Mother Earth.

Five and six sorties in a day were the norm on the bombing and rocketing range, and we finished the course with seventy-five adrenaline-packed flying hours in the two months.

AWI Course at RNAS Lossiemouth. Landing nine Hunter T.8s in July 1960.

Finishing the AWI course, I looked forward to getting an appointment as AWI to a squadron flying the new de Havilland Sea Vixen aircraft. This seemed very likely since there was only one squadron left still flying the old Sea Venom. However, this was 891 Squadron, the outfit I had previously requested to join to stay with friends from my original fighter 'course'. Their Lordships at the Admiralty now fulfilled my stated wish, though of course all my previous contemporaries had now moved on. But my year as AWI with 891, shore-based at the naval air station at Yeovilton and with twelve Sea Venom crews, was totally satisfying. Although now the 'junior' Fleet Air Arm all-weather fighter squadron in equipment terms, we ran a hectic programme, practising weaponry on the Scottish ranges while deployed to Lossiemouth and at Yeovilton, the inevitable AI (airborne interception) exercises, day and night, and, higher up the enjoyment scale, a return to some formation aerobatics.

The squadron CO, Lt Cdr 'Mickey' Brown led our small aeros team, which toured the various naval air stations that year, 1961, with Lt Doug Borrowman and myself as wingmen. Flying symmetric formation when offset from the aircraft centre line, as in the Venom, is a bit of a trick, since your position in relation to the aircraft in front must vary in distance and angle, depending on which side you join. But, once again, the manoeuvrability and lightness on the controls of the Sea Venom made it a pleasant exercise (see colour plate 17).

891 Squadron's aerobatics team at Yeovilton in June 1961. Left to right: Borrowman, Eagles, Brown (CO).

During my time at Yeovilton I continued with my enjoyment of beekeeping and had reasonable success. I note that much of my correspondence with Dad over the next few years was on the subject of various problems of swarming, bee diseases and hive making. During the summer months it was necessary to 'go through' the bees once a week to prevent swarming and I found it a fascinating and calming sport. I kept my bees on some waste ground on the edge of Yeovilton airfield, not far from the village church. I recall stopping to see that they were in good order as I drove my great friend, Observer Andy Haughton, to his wedding at that church, where I was to act as his best man. This event, at that time, did not have the same calming effect on Andy.

In July 1961 I was sent as AWI to the All Weather Fighter School at Yeovilton and so finally got my wish to fly the Sea Vixen. The Vixen had had an unhappy development. It had originally been designed as an all-weather fighter for both the RAF and the navy in competition with the Gloster Javelin, back in the balmy days when the defence budget allowed several competitive designs to be produced for each requirement. The prototype DH.110 (later to become the Sea Vixen) flew first on 26 September 1951 and in September 1952, during a display at the Farnborough Air Show, it broke up in front of the crowd during a rolling pull-out from a dive, killing the crew, John Derry and Tony Richards, and also twenty-eight spectators. After major redesign of the wing structure and other changes, including to the stick feel system, the development of the navy version continued and in April 1956 the first arrested landing was made on HMS *Ark Royal*, flown by naval test pilot Cdr Stan Orr, with Dennis Higton, later to become a great friend, in the observers' seat, the 'coal hole'.

The Sea Vixen was a significant step up in performance from the navy's earlier fighters. Its maximum speed at low level was 600 knots (at less than full power) and at height it was transonic in a dive, reaching around Mach 1.1 diving at 15 to 20 degrees, or Mach 1.3 pointing straight down! It turned well and would take quite rough handling near the stall without fear of departing into a spin.

It carried the Firestreak infrared-seeking missile and an interception radar, the AI 18, which was a reliable performer and was controlled by the observer in the coal hole. He had a view of the pilot's cockpit through an aperture in his left cockpit wall and there was a small external window by his right shoulder. The view through this was said to be like a television with the vertical hold gone wrong. The pilot's cockpit was offset to the left under a sliding canopy, which, together with a vee windscreen, gave good

The de Havilland
Sea Vixen Mk1s
of 'Fred's Five'
aerobatics team at
Yeovilton in May
1962.

external view. There were several excellent innovations, which made deck work easier. One was a nosewheel steering system controlled by a wheel below the pilot's left forearm. This made accurate manoeuvring on the flight deck very much easier than with the asymmetric use of wheel brakes as in the previous generation aircraft. And there was an excellent windscreen rain-blowing system, which cleared the windscreen exterior to maintain forward vision in grotty weather.

The aircraft was pretty easy to fly during a typical airborne interception exercise and during air-to-ground weapon delivery, but in fighter manoeuvring it was a little heavy on the stick both in pitch and roll. Certainly in comparison with the Hunter we had used at Lossiemouth for fighter tactics training, the Vixen was very tiring and I often reverted to both hands on the stick when pulling through long turns. Another area that was slightly uncomfortable was control in the pitch plane at low level, particularly at very high speed, above 500 knots. Tailplane response always felt a bit delayed so that control of height was slightly imprecise. Some years later, when flying both the Vixen and the Buccaneer (designed specifically for high-speed, low-level flight) during my time at Boscombe Down, I was able to compare the two and it was no contest!

The Vixen had been designed without guns, its main air-to-air weapon being the Firestreak missile. However, it was also fitted with a retractable launcher under the nose designed to carry twenty-four air-to-air 2in rockets, but to my knowledge this system was never used by the squadrons. I believe the accuracy was so poor that it would have been unsafe to carry out practice firings against towed targets. The same 2in rockets were carried in under-wing rocket pods though and were effective in the air-to-ground role.

The task at the AWF School at Yeovilton (766 Squadron) was training new crews to use all aspects of the Vixen's capabilities, i.e. the AI radar, the Firestreak missile system, and air-to-ground weapons, rockets and bombs. The CO, Lt Cdr Peter Reynolds, was a most amiable man and well liked by staff and students. He was also a graduate of the Empire Test Pilots' School and I cornered him early in my time there for advice on how best to prepare for an application. He was very supportive and described the attractions of working in the Naval Test Squadron at Boscombe Down. It was possible there to fly just about any aircraft type on the base, he said, and he went on to recall checking out in the Blackburn Beverley, an enormous and ugly freighter with a vast fuselage. 'It was like flying a council house from the bathroom window …'

Peter was tasked in 1961 to work up a navy aerobatic team to perform at the Farnborough Air Show the following year. When I arrived at the squadron in July 1961, to replace my old friend Simon Idiens as AWI, I found he had been flying as number two in Pete's provisional team and I was invited to take his place. The team consisted of five aircraft with six crews available and quickly became known as 'Fred's Five'. In early 1962 we began to practise whenever there was a gap in the training programme and then in the summer of that year we started a routine of flying early with an aeros practice before each day's routine instruction programme.

The Vixen was by no means an ideal aircraft for formation aerobatics, at least not from the pilots' point of view. As mentioned earlier, it had heavy stick forces, particularly in pitch, so it was a sweaty occupation. Sometimes I had to take my left hand off the throttle momentarily to help pull the stick back. And the offset cockpit meant that we all had to learn different relative positions depending on which side of the man in front we were flying at the time. From a spectator viewpoint though it was a spectacular aircraft with its twin boom layout, and to increase the interest still more we had de Havilland design a modification to produce coloured smoke. Each aircraft was modified to carry an additional small external fuel tank that fed coloured dye to the jet pipe via some ugly external plumbing. The system was switched on and off from the stick weapons trigger and worked well until, during the Farnborough show itself, the tank on my aircraft burst and dropped neat blue dye over the car park and part of the spectator area. The Admiralty was swamped with claims for damage to car paintwork and some of the crowd developed 'Fred's freckles'.

The aircraft may not have been ideal but as a leader Pete Reynolds was exceptionally smooth and the crews loved it. Our first display was at the opening of Speke Airport in Liverpool on 26 May 1962 and we made ten more displays before the main one at Farnborough that year. There was a

They're blue Charlie. Looks like Fred's freckles.

certain amount of fooling about in the cockpit during the practice and sometimes during the displays. When I hadn't heard from my observer, 'Horace' Morris, for a while, I would press the test button on the audio warning system occasionally to keep up his adrenaline quotient. And he in turn would occasionally get his arm through the gap between the cockpits and press my oxygen test button, which had the effect of blowing me up like the Michelin man.

During my time at Yeovilton, and encouraged by Pete Reynolds, I applied for the Empire Test Pilots' Course at Farnborough. Interviews were held there yearly and I recall facing four or five RAF officers who asked the usual searching questions to test aviation knowledge and individual motivation. The one navy test pilot on the board, Cdr Mike Crosley (whom I discovered later was the CO of the Naval Test Squadron at Boscombe Down) said very little during the interview until towards the end when he chipped in with, 'OK, you seem to have a reasonable flying background, but do you have any other interests; can you play the trumpet or sing?'

In August 1962 in Yeovil I married Raewyn Leach, whom I had first met on board the liner *Rangitoto* while returning from my two-year stint with the Australian Fleet Air Arm. The first months of our married life were somewhat hectic, with daily early morning departures for the aerobatic team practices and night-flying student instruction. And shortly afterwards, in October, I was appointed as AWI to 892 Squadron, also flying the Sea Vixen, and in November we embarked in HMS *Hermes*, en route to the Far East.

Flying from the deck in the Vixen was not the enjoyable experience I had expected and known in the smaller Venom. The Vixen was bigger, of course; there was less margin for error either side of the flight deck centre line and launch and landing speeds were some 15–20 knots faster. Stability on the approach at landing speeds seemed near neutral and lateral control was far from crisp. By day these characteristics were not obvious but by night, and in comparison with the later Buccaneer, I found the Vixen a bit more challenging. Many friends at that time, who did much more deck time in it than I did, disagree with my opinion and it is perhaps because I was called back to the UK after only three months of flying that I never become a fan of the Vixen at night at sea.

Off Singapore I made a common mistake. After start-up on deck, in the hot and humid conditions there, I put the cabin conditioning to full cold while sitting at idle power in an effort to keep cool. On the catapult I failed to readjust it to normal, in spite of previous warnings, and as the catapult fired, the cockpit fogged out and I couldn't see either out of the cockpit or the instruments on the panel in front of me. I fumbled around with my left hand searching for the cockpit air temperature control while pulling back slightly – or at least I thought I was doing it gently – to get the nose up for a climb away. My observer, Flt Lt Dorman-Jackson, a very capable RAF navigator on loan to the navy, was able to get his eyes much closer to his instrument panel and began chanting out the reducing airspeed figures. This news encouraged me to push the stick forward to reduce what was obviously a startling nose-up attitude, and this coincided thankfully with success with the cockpit temperature selector. I was always content to endure the heat while waiting for the catapult after that.

4

Empire Test Pilots' School

In the middle of January 1963, with *Hermes* in Hong Kong, I was sent back to the UK to join the next course at the Empire Test Pilots' School at Farnborough. I was sorry to be missing the ship's planned visit to Japan but this was the course I had so much hoped to be able to join. The school had started in 1943 at Boscombe Down in Wiltshire, when there had been a worryingly high loss rate among the test crews of the experimental aircraft in those war years. It was opened up to pilots from abroad from the second course, in 1944, when the students included Chinese, Americans, Australians, Dutch and Polish.

In 1963, of the twenty-six students who assembled at the school in the snow at Farnborough in late January, fifteen were from the RAF, three from the Fleet Air Arm, two from the US Navy, and one each from the US Air Force, Indian Air Force, Canadian Air Force, Italian Air Force, Australian Air Force, and one (the first ever) from the British Army. Our course, for the first time, included a separate syllabus for rotary wing (i.e. helicopter pilots), of which we had two from the RAF, one from the navy and the aforementioned student from the army. Our academic standards varied widely. Several had degrees in engineering or mathematics, but for most of us our schooling had stopped at 'A' level. For the first two weeks we were given lectures on maths, mechanics and aerodynamics and I invested in a 'teach yourself calculus' book. In 1963 the calculator and the home computer were yet to appear and slide rules and typewriters were the tools of the moment. After this attempt to get us all up to a workable standard, we began the routine of a half-day in the classroom and a half in the air.

The school had thirteen aircraft, all of which were RAF types with the exception of the Vickers Viscount airliner, the navy Supermarine Scimitar and the Slingsby T.34 glider. The Scimitar spent most of its time in pieces though we were all able to fly it at least once. Our five instructors, or tutors as they were known in the school, were all graduates of ETPS and had all done a tour of test-flying duty at one of the Ministry of Defence establishments. We were split into syndicates and assigned to a tutor, who guided us through the various exercises that built up in complexity as the year proceeded. Early in the course our Australian student went against the house rules and while doing his familiarisation flying on the English Electric Canberra aircraft carried out a 'touch and go' landing in crosswind conditions. The school's Canberra had an early standard of Avon engine that was prone to stalling if opened up quickly in a crosswind; one engine stalled and he pirouetted along the runway, ending up on the grass with the landing gear sheared off. He was not hurt but was quietly withdrawn.

There was an interesting exercise associated with this, our only accident on the year's course. Four or five of us had been watching the touch and go from the crew room window over a mug of coffee and so had witnessed the crash. Our tutor, Sqn Ldr Eddie Rigg, straightaway asked us all to separate and write down exactly what we saw. The difference in the detail we each reported was significant, which was surprising since all concerned were familiar with the everyday scenes of landing aircraft. So one of the first lessons we learned at ETPS was the trustworthiness or otherwise of eyewitness reports of high-speed events.

The ETPS fleet at Farnborough in 1963. The Scimitar was in pieces in the hangar.

The school syllabus covered a series of flying exercises designed to determine some aspect of an aircraft's behaviour or performance. The main methods of recording results or observations were by scribbling down notes on a kneepad or, entering the world of hi-tech, speaking into a tape or wire recorder. It was a common sight to see someone land in the Piston Provost and open up the small compartment in the fuselage that held the wire recorder, to reveal a bird's nest of recording wire that had jumped off the spool. The scribbled note was best, but then spare pencils were a must and each was best tied to your flying suit with a length of string. The luxury of data recorders and telemetry was still to come.

After getting the data by whatever means, the final stages of the exercise were to reduce it to standard conditions – or adjust the results mathematically to what could be expected on a 'standard' day – and finally to write a report. This would be reviewed by the tutor and returned with 'helpful notes' in red ink. Attempts to introduce humour into the report were not favoured, regardless of appropriateness. A previous course student had written of his assessment of the Fairey Gannet, 'Entry to the cockpit is difficult. Recommend it be made impossible.'

One of the least comfortable exercises on the course was spinning and we were all given a demonstration of the most severe form, inverted spinning, by tutor Eddie Rigg. The inverted spinning exercise results in 'eyeballs out' G-forces and Eddie was the only man believed to actually enjoy it. The two-seat Hunter we used for this exercise was specially modified by the inclusion of a 'spinning panel' fitted in place of the usual instrument panel in front of the right-hand seat, normally occupied by the student. This panel held two or three instruments that were non-standard to help with spin recognition and recovery. One of these was a single pointer altimeter, marked clearly to indicate when you were below 10,000ft – the altitude at which you should eject if attempts to recover from the spin had sadly been unsuccessful. This was a 4in-diameter gauge, positioned directly in front of the student's face and which therefore, one noted, tended to reflect the grimaces on the said face during the inverted spin. It was good sport to watch our fellow students walking out to the Hunter with Sqn Ldr Rigg and to note the difference in facial colour on return. Our USAF pilot, Maj. Bill Pogue (who later orbited the Earth for weeks in Skylab 3) when asked 'how it went' on his return from this exercise, said, 'Man! It was all teeth and eyeballs!'

A memorable aspect of the school was the trust that was put in the students to prepare responsibly for flying aircraft with which they were not familiar.

No blindfold cockpit checks here. We picked up the pilots' notes for each type as we were assigned an exercise in it and studied them in our own time. The staff included two non-test pilot qualified flying instructors who unveiled the mysteries of flying twin-engined aircraft to those of us who were only single-engine experienced (the Sea Vixen didn't count as a twin because with engines side by side on the centre line, a single engine failure hardly affected handling at all). The Canberra and Meteor were much more of a handful with one engine out, and the four-engined Viscount merited two trips with a test pilot instructor before being allowed to solo it.

The value of the ETPS course was certainly greater than the sum of its parts. The techniques that we learned, to extract data from the aircraft being tested, were the bread and butter. But at least as important was the recognition, when reading a trial instruction, of the areas of a test that were likely to bring the aircraft close to some degree of risk. At the school we were able to discuss the planned techniques with the tutors and with the other course members. Several years later the school began to include flight test engineers as students, making it possible to develop teams, with a test pilot and a flight test engineer, to share all aspects of the preparation for each data gathering flight, as well as the processing of the resulting data after it. Other benefits, of course, included the contacts inevitably made, which were maintained during the students' subsequent careers. Of the twenty-six students on the 1963 course, six went on to be chief test pilots or the service or Civil Aviation Authority equivalent, two became officers of flag rank in one of the services and, as mentioned above, one joined the corps of astronauts.

As part of the course we visited each of the UK aircraft manufacturer's sites in turn, where we could see their latest projects and be briefed by their own test pilots on progress. These trips were much looked forward to as they normally entailed an overnight stay and some heavy socialising. The school's Viscount was a very handy means of getting around to the various company airfields. We flew to Belfast to see the new heavylift turboprop freighter, the Shorts Belfast, and we wondered at the size and the likely drag problems. Among others, we visited English Electric at Warton, for briefings on TSR-2, de Havilland at Hatfield to see Comet production, Blackburns at Holme-on-Spalding-Moor for an update on the Buccaneer, and Hawkers for a briefing on the new VTOL project, the Harrier.

The hosts always gave a centrepiece presentation on some flight-testing subject they were currently involved with and, as is normal on such occasions, one student would be briefed beforehand to ask the first question after the lecture, to avoid any ugly silence. On our visit to Rolls-Royce at Hucknall we were given a presentation on the then new technique of cooling turbine blades by introducing a cooling air flow through drillings in turbine disc and blade. Our nominated question-asker had unfortunately given in to slumber during the presentation but was brought back to life with a sharp elbow. He stood up somewhat dazed and after thanking the speaker for an excellent talk, asked if he could say a few words about the new technique of cooling turbine blades through drillings. This became known thereafter as 'doing a Smith', the name having been changed here to protect the guilty.

The final exercise of the course was, and is, the 'preview'. Each student is assigned an aircraft, ideally one with which he is not overly familiar, and is required to treat it as one given to him for eight hours' flying in which he is to examine all aspects and write a report on its suitability and acceptability for its role. These days the ETPS is able to 'borrow' aircraft from the fleets of other test pilot schools or from other agencies to fulfil this role and thereby provide the student with totally unfamiliar hardware. For preview I was given the Viscount, which, although quite dissimilar to anything I had much experience in, I had flown before on an auto-pilot assessment exercise at the school. My wife, Raewyn, was doing the typing of this final report, but let me down badly in the middle of it by disappearing into hospital to produce our first child, Simon, in late November. But graduating well, and a healthy heir, combined to make a happy ending to the year. (A coffee-stained copy of the first page of the ETPS final exam paper is in Appendix 1.)

Although the time at ETPS was action-packed I was able to find time to continue my hobby of beekeeping. During our year at Farnborough we rented a house in Camberley that had a small, walled garden and I took two hives there. We were fairly close to a large patch of heather at Frensham Pond and we took the bees there for the month of August that year for a crop of heather honey. I found beekeeping a highly relaxing hobby in which I could get fully absorbed and enjoyed the total change of scene.

5

Boscombe Down

After the Empire Test Pilots' School, the UK students were assigned a three-year tour at one of the three main government establishments involved with test flying: Bedford, Farnborough or Boscombe Down. I think most of us would have chosen the Royal Aircraft Establishment at Bedford as a preference since it was the home of Aero Flight, the unit closest to pure research flying, and it held the most exotic prototype aircraft in the country. But only one pilot per course was expected to have that honour and it turned out to be John Farley, later chief test pilot at BAe Dunsfold and best known for his development work on the Harrier. Those exotic types in the Aero Flight fleet when John went there in 1964 included the HP.115, the slender delta research aircraft; the Fairey FD2, a supersonic research aircraft that took the absolute speed record over 1,000mph (achieving 1,132mph) in 1956; the Shorts SB.5, researching different theories on wing and tail design for the new Lightning fighter; the Hunting H.126, experimental blown flap aircraft, later lent to NASA; and the vertical take-off P.1127 and Kestrel aircraft from which the Harrier was developed. Mouth-watering stuff.

One more of our number, Flt Lt Jim Baerselman, also went to RAE Bedford, but to the Blind Landing Experimental Unit (BLEU) where in that year, 1964, it achieved the first fully automatic landing using a BAC One-Eleven. But most of the rest of us reported for duty at the Aircraft and Armament Experimental Establishment (A&AEE) at Boscombe Down in Wiltshire. Here the aircraft types that were due to enter service for the UK services were checked for suitability and conformity with agreed specifications, and in-service types had modifications tested and approved. There were five test squadrons here, A, B, C, D and E, looking after fighters, bombers, naval aircraft, helicopters and transports respectively; C Squadron was manned by Fleet Air Arm test crews, D Squadron by helicopter pilots from all three services and all the other squadrons by RAF test crews.

The commanding officer of C Squadron was Cdr Geoff Higgs, a very experienced navy test pilot who was admirably decisive. He had commanded the first embarked Scimitar Squadron in HMS *Victorious* during my time in the same ship and quite apart from dealing with the difficulties of the initially temperamental Scimitar, I thought he had also handled the eight or so pilots in that squadron in excellent fashion. All of them were prima donnas, since theirs was the first of the big transonic fighter squadrons to be squeezed aboard those compact British carriers, and all of them had been specially selected for that honour. In C Squadron he had six test pilots, including the two new boys, Brian Bullivant and myself, and six observers. The squadron aircraft when we arrived in January 1964 were a Blackburn Buccaneer Mk1, a Fairey Gannet, two de Havilland Sea Vixens, a Mk1 and a Mk2, and the only surviving Bolton Paul Sea Balliol. The Balliol was a piston-engined naval training aircraft; a side-by-side two-seater, fitted with a hook that the squadron used for ferrying individuals or spares to carriers during deck trials.

My first trip in C Squadron was in the back seat of a Buccaneer Mk1 with Lt Alan Deacon driving. The Mk1, though underpowered, was an impressive performer at very low level and Alan threw it around at about 50ft over Lyme Bay, determined to impress the new boy. This aim was certainly achieved when he pulled into a 6g turn, 550 knots at that height, to demonstrate the

C Squadron Fleet at Boscombe Down in May 1964, comprising Sea Vixen Mk1, Sea Balliol, Fairey Gannet AEW.3 and Buccaneer Mk2.

engines' tendency to surge under those conditions. Sitting between the intakes I was treated to the full machine-gun-like sound effects from both engines.

At the end of the previous year, the Sea Vixen Mk2 had entered service, with a new air-to-air missile system, the Red Top, replacing the Mk1's Firestreak. To find room for the extra avionics that the missile system needed, and to increase fuel tankage, the aircraft's distinctive twin booms had been extended forward over and beyond the wing. C Squadron had been allocated one of the early Mk2s, XN684, for development of this missile system, and this work continued throughout my three years in the squadron. The aircraft itself was 3,500lb heavier than the previous model and the joke in the Fleet Air Arm was that it was to be re-engined with the Concorde's engines to bring it back to the performance of the Mk1. In fact, its performance and handling as a result of the changes were virtually indistinguishable from the Mk1; very slightly more stable directionally and in pitch. As well as the new missile system, the Vixen Mk2 had an auto-throttle system fitted, specifically to lighten the piloting load for deck landings and so reduce the white-knuckle factor on black nights.

The Red Top missile-system development flying was demanding but pretty dull stuff. Many sorties consisted of taking the aircraft to the missile range at Aberporth in Cardigan Bay on the Welsh west coast to achieve a specific set of flight conditions on a safe firing heading and with the aircraft radar locked on to an unmanned Jindivik target. Achieving all the required parameters of airspeed, height, g, attitude and heading at the same time required great concentration; the data was collected on an on-board tape arrangement so that system performance and behaviour could be analysed on the ground.

It was on returning from one of these Red Top development flights at Aberporth in September 1964 that I saw, as I taxied in, the sad sight of the second TSR-2 prototype's fuselage lying on its side by the C Squadron hangar door, still strapped to its Queen Mary trailer, which had rolled over. Its tow truck, still upright, appeared to have turned very tightly back on itself, presumably to position the trailer for unloading close to the door. The TSR-2 programme was the UK's most critical aerospace project at this time and this was a very serious blow, which delayed the preparation of the second prototype for flight significantly. And the whole project was later scrapped anyhow after the first prototype had flown only twenty-four sorties, and this second prototype never flew.

In C Squadron we had half our hangar commandeered for the assembly of the first prototype TSR-2 by working parties from Vickers and English Electric.

A temporary wall was constructed dividing the hangar into two, each half with its own doors. An amusing incident occurred during the assembly of the first prototype. Security was obviously high around the whole hangar, but one Monday morning when we arrived for work we found a small, neat hole had been punched through the dividing wall, which was made of some cement sheet material, some 10ft above floor level. We learned later that the TSR-2 assembly had reached the 'hydraulics on' stage over the weekend and that a coupling had given up its job and allowed a unit of some sort to fire off through the wall. In good old navy fashion some wits had pushed a stepladder against the wall on our side, ringed the 6in diameter hole and painted the caption 'TSR-2 assembly progress viewing'.

The squadron was given a second Sea Vixen Mk2 for various other Vixen trials, most of which were more absorbing for the crew. These included handling the aircraft with new stores under the wings, streaming towed targets and exploring the feasibility of in-flight refuelling from various types of tanker.

In-flight refuelling is an enjoyable challenge to the pilot, provided that you are not desperately short of fuel when you start (a situation that concentrates the mind wonderfully). On the Sea Vixen, like the BAC Lightning, the refuelling probe protruded from the leading edge of the wing some 7 or 8ft out to the left of the pilot. The tanker streams a refuelling hose, on the end of which is a drogue or 'basket' into which you plan to push the business end of your receiving probe. The procedure is to fly your receiver aircraft to a position where the end of the probe is some 6 to 10ft behind the basket, and pause. This positioning is helped by having a mark, real or imaginary, on the tanker fuselage or wing that is straight ahead of you, and which is that same 7 or 8ft to the right of the trailing hose. Then, keeping further control movements to a minimum and keeping eyes on the aiming mark, you add power to achieve an overtake speed of about 5 knots. With peripheral vision you note if the probe makes contact, or the amount and direction of the error if you miss. Meanwhile, the basket might be moving up and down through turbulence and any aileron input you make to keep lined up with the aiming mark will move the probe above or below the line of the basket. On a reasonable day you will hit the basket three times out of five attempts. When the probe enters the cone-shaped basket it is led to its apex and the impact forces the probe end-fitting to lock into a spring-loaded hose fitting. Once that contact is made, the fuel can be made to flow by moving forward, so pushing the hose forward a little way back into its housing in the tanker, which makes an appropriate switch. To break the lock the receiver simply throttles back, pulling the hose out to the receiving position again and then further aft until the lock is broken.

The various tanker types produce different degrees of downwash or slipstream over the receiver aircraft, depending on the tanker shape and whether you are refuelling from a pod under the tanker's wing or from a main centre line hose installation. This slipstream might cause the basket itself to bounce around or make flying in that close formation position difficult. In November 1964 we investigated refuelling with the Vickers Valiant as a tanker, and in May 1965 we flew both Vixen and Buccaneer against the Victor tanker then being developed. In January 1966 the Air Ministry was considering whether or not it could use its Armstrong Whitworth Argosy freighter aircraft in the tanker role and we were asked to check the feasibility of refuelling the Sea Vixen from this much slower beast (see colour plate 18). The Argosy was fitted externally with an in-flight refuelling pod (from which it streamed a refuelling hose) on the lower port side of its box-like fuselage and, as it happened, the offset of this pod from the Argosy's centre line was dimensionally the same as the offset of the Vixen's in-flight refuelling probe to the left of the cockpit. So we were able to drive straight up the Argosy's easily discernible centre line. But the Argosy's maximum speed with the refuelling drogue streamed was only around 200 knots, so we knew that control at that low airspeed would be soggy and would make things difficult (normal refuelling speed with the bigger tankers was 250 to 280 knots). However, both with and without the Vixen's flaps extended, control into the basket was acceptable, but with the low airspeed we could only rarely get the probe to lock into the basket; the lack of drag at that low airspeed allowed the basket to simply bounce away. The Argosy was therefore not to be included in the tanker list (see Appendix 2 for a copy of the test report).

The Buccaneer was first designed with a retractable refuelling probe on the aircraft's nose just to the right of the windscreen. This position appeared to be ideal, since the probe end was clearly in the pilot's view. However, the probe was so short that, when extended, its end was only 2 or 3ft from the skin of the nose. During testing in 1963, the Boscombe test pilots had found that as they flew the probe end towards the basket, the wash from the Buccaneer nose pushed the basket away to the right, making the task virtually impossible. This had been reported back to the navy as an unacceptable feature requiring redesign, but the first Buccaneer Mk1 squadron had already been formed at Lossiemouth and was waiting for a clearance to carry out in-flight refuelling. The navy felt that the Boscombe test pilots were probably being too academic and sent down a 'more realistic, operational pilot' to look at the problem. The operational visitor was no more able to make refuelling contacts than the Boscombe pilots, though, and a longer, fixed probe was designed that increased drag, of course, but was workable.

We received our first Buccaneer Mk2 in May 1964 and I was made project pilot for its introduction into service. The Mk1, with its de Havilland Gyron Junior engines, was well liked in service in its role as an under the radar strike aircraft. It incorporated some new features such as area ruling, where the fuselage is 'pinched' at the wing junction to keep the overall cross sectional area smoothly progressive as it grows and reduces along its length. However, the Mk1 was somewhat underpowered and bar humour had it that it relied on the curvature of the Earth to get airborne. This was brought home to me when I flew a Meteor T.7 aircraft as photographic chase for the CO, who was to do anti-spin parachute streaming checks on our Buccaneer Mk1 prior to some slow-speed handling evaluation. I was briefed to do a formation take-off as his wingman. We lined up on the main runway, we both opened up to full power for engine checks and the boss gave the signal for brakes off. I was somewhat surprised to find that my 1944 vintage jet immediately shot ahead and I had to throttle well back to wait for the navy's new nuclear bomber to catch up. It is only fair to add that once up and away, the Mk1, with its slightly unreliable Gyron Junior engines, was very hard to catch and was very comfortable at 600 knots at 50ft.

The replacing of the two 7,000lb-thrust Gyron Junior engines on the Mk1 with two 11,255lb thrust Rolls-Royce Spey engines naturally transformed the Mk2 version. Maximum range was increased by nearly 80 per cent and touch-and-go landings could be performed comfortably on one engine. The other main changes were to the electrical system, the previous 28v DC arrangement being replaced by two 30kva AC generators, and to the weapons system. Our first Mk2 was a converted Mk1, XK527, 'handmade by Florentine craftsmen', and I enjoyed many interesting hours in her. The bigger engines made her significantly more noisy in the cockpit than the Mk1s until Blackburns increased the amount of cockpit noise insulation. The only area in which the Mk2 was inferior to the Mk1 was in pitch and yaw stability at very high indicated air speed. Above 550 knots (maximum permitted was 600 knots) a very light, pitch oscillation was just discernible and directionally the aircraft was not as tight. The Spey engines had required a significant increase in the size of the air intakes and no doubt this change was responsible for this very slight degradation.

For the first major test of the Mk2 we took '527 to the RAF Airfield at Idris near Tripoli in Libya for hot-weather trials. It's amazing now to remember that the UK had an RAF base out in the Libyan desert that we could simply contact and tell we were coming to operate at for a month or so. The airfield was built out on the sand and on one occasion we did high-power engine runs on the end of the runway, checking radio bay cooling, and found that the engine jet exhaust had created a hole in the desert about 25ft deep. In thirty days there we flew twenty-nine sorties and thirty-four hours, doing mainly engine and equipment flight tests in temperatures around 35°C.

One incident there illustrates the frailty of the human as observer. For one sortie we had turned off the cooling unit that was designed to prevent overheating in the avionics bay to determine whether and how any of the avionic components would malfunction in the event of a cooling unit failure. To generate maximum heating the sortie required a long high-speed run at low level over the desert. Our main concern was that the pitch auto-stabiliser might 'cook' and produce a spurious nose-down input. The unit did indeed cook and I returned and reported an uncalled for nose-up input. The engineers examined the on-board recorder information and pointed out that the failure had actually produced a nose-down input that had been swamped by an instinctive nose-up pull.

We used the same low-level route at fairly high speed (550 knots) on nine or ten occasions. We followed a road or track to the south-west that Mike Lithgow had apparently used when he set up a world speed record in the Swift in September 1953. The scenery was spectacular; red undulating desert for about fifteen minutes and then the track led into a steep-sided valley of red rocks in the sides of which were cave entrances, the homes of local troglodytes who could be seen running out on to terraces to check on the noise. After doing our turnaround at the end of the run and settling down into the valley again, at 50 to 100ft, I had the unforgettable sight of a man standing on a plateau above and hurling a stick at us! An understandable reaction to a crude intrusion into their largely untouched world.

The RAF station at Idris had originally been built by the Italian Air Force and had been in use during the Second World War. The officers' mess had clearly been quite a luxurious set-up, with much use of marble and large areas for al fresco dining among attractive fountains. It is the only place in the world that I have seen handholds alongside the urinal stalls in the toilets, allegedly to steady the attendees at mess dinners. We had the use of an RAF Land Rover for our off-duty hours and were able to visit the fabulous ancient Roman town of Leptis Magna on the Mediterranean coast.

The Buccaneer was a complicated aircraft with high-pressure air tapped off the two engines and fed to the wing, flaps and tailplane flap to provide boundary layer control (BLC). This 'blow system' allowed the designers to plan a high-wing loading aircraft, optimised for high-speed, low-level manoeuvres, while still making it possible to achieve an acceptably low landing speed on to the carrier. To illustrate the effectiveness of the blow system, the aircraft's normal approach speed with blow working was 130 knots, but with blow switched off speed had to be increased to around 164 knots to generate the same lift for the same aircraft weight.

As a test pilot at Boscombe Down in the mid-1960s it was still possible to beg rides in aircraft in other squadrons (that luxury was soon to be lost). The rationale was that by gaining experience in a wide variety of different aircraft types, the pilot would be better able to evaluate, and perhaps recommend change to, projects with which he was involved. The opposing view was that when flying unfamiliar types, the chances of dealing quickly with any emergency that might arise were reduced. But in this relaxed atmosphere I was able to fly some of A Squadron's fighters such as the Lightning, Javelin and Hunter, B Squadron's bombers such as the Canberra and Vulcan, D Squadron helicopters, including the Whirlwind, Alouette and Wessex and E Squadron's Dominie, Argosy and ancient Anson. Did these opportunities really help to do the job? Not so much, perhaps, in my time at Boscombe, where the emphasis was on finding ways to make acceptable what was already designed and virtually delivered. But certainly in my future years at British Aerospace Warton, where we were to start in some cases with a clean sheet of paper and the design was not yet always set in stone.

As regards flying many different types in the same month – and my own maximum at Boscombe was fourteen, though fellow naval test pilot Peter Banfield achieved twenty-one – I believe the defence against the cry of unfamiliarity was preparation and the use of checklists. Strangely, there is a danger when flying the same single type solidly for years that checklists are dispensed with, or at least rushed as a result of familiarity, and vital actions are missed. (My fourteen types in one month were: Buccaneer Mk2, Lightning, Meteor T.7, Javelin, Canberra, Sea Vixen, Sea Balliol, Jet Provost, Hunter GA.11, MU-2, Rapide, Argosy, Vulcan, and Whirlwind HAS.7.)

In March 1965 we began to prepare for deck trials for the Buccaneer Mk2, initially with simulated deck-landing practice at Boscombe Down. With the Mk1 version, the comparatively low maximum thrust of the engines meant that during the approach to a carrier landing the engines were operating at 85–90 per cent power on the approach. At this power setting, the air pressure, at the point on the engine where it was tapped off for boundary layer control, was high. As the pilot made typical frequent throttle movements during the approach, blow pressure remained good, even at the lowest engine revs seen. With the Mk2 though, the thrust/blow ratio had been changed. The Spey engine was so powerful that, on the approach, the engine setting was well back in the available power range and this meant that the blow pressure, tapped off the fourth stage of the engine compressors, could drop to a dangerously low level during 'throttle jockeying'. If pressures dropped below around 15psi, the slots through which the air was directed over the wing, flaps and tailplane flap became 'unchoked' and wing and tail lift would be reduced suddenly. You could hear this sudden change in airflow over the wing from the cockpit. For a while there was talk of seeking to change the point of air tapping to a higher pressure point on the engine but this would have been a hugely complicated and expensive change. The eventual fix was simply to use full airbrake for the approach to increase drag and so use a higher power setting on the approach. The downside of this (and there's usually a downside) was the accompanying airbrake buffet that you then had to live with throughout the approach. To have a permanent buffet in a low-speed flight regime is not a good thing since, of course, it tends to mask the buffet that might be the natural warning of impending stall. However, this was eventually determined to be the best way forward, and indeed in squadron service this feature never proved a problem. Writing up these memories of the thrust/blow ratio problem fifty years later, the item seems trivial when recalling that the difficulty was overcome simply with a procedure change. But at the time a lot of time and experimentation was devoted to it.

In March 1965 we took the first two pre-production standard Buccaneer Mk2s to sea in HMS *Ark Royal*, operating in the English Channel. Geoff Higgs, the CO, Derek Whitehead, Blackburn's chief test pilot, and myself, plus three observers from C Squadron did the flying under the control of the performance engineers from Boscombe, Dennis Higton and Dennis Sharp. The aim was to determine minimum catapult launch speeds at various weights, minimum approach speeds and to examine approaches without 'blow'. The trials took a week and each crew enjoyed around twenty-five

Buccaneer Mk2 deck trials on HMS *Ark Royal* in 1965.

deck landings in that time. There were no nasty surprises, most of the carrier suitability aspects of the aircraft having been sorted out during the previous trials with the Mk1. The ship was ours for the trials period – it was doing trials of its own and there were no other aircraft embarked – so we were able to make rapid progress.

To achieve a high sortie rate, the typical routine was to catapult launch with bombs under the wing or in the bomb bay and with full under-wing fuel tanks, then jettison the bombs and dump the fuel to get down to maximum landing weight quickly to carry out touch and go landings at the speeds being examined. On one embarrassing day I launched with bombs under the wings three times in quick succession, jettisoning them immediately after launch, to achieve maximum landing weight quickly. For my next launch that day I changed to an aircraft with under-wing tanks to carry out a similar check, but stupidly dropped a fuel tank as well as the bombs immediately after launch (as on the previous launches, I selected 'clear wings' instead of specifying the stations to be jettisoned). Both tanks should have gone but one jettison circuit was defective and the landing had to be done in an unbalanced configuration.

The Buccaneer has a very high inertia in pitch and so if you get it pitching at low airspeed you need large tailplane movements to control it.

Consequently, the catapult launch arrangements called for a nose-up launch attitude to cut out the need for the pilot to have to make a significant nose-up pitch demand at the low airspeeds that exist immediately post-launch. A tailplane trim setting was first calculated by the designers and then confirmed or refined in test, which allowed the pilot to leave his hands off the stick during the catapult launch and find it in trim without the need to make a stick input for three or four seconds – or even longer – after the launch. Blackburns also devised a fairing for the aircraft's under-wing fuel tanks that reduced drag to very low levels but also further reduced pitch stability and made it even more necessary to avoid getting the aircraft pitching at low speeds (see colour plate 19).

The aircraft's stick was mass balanced so that the acceleration experienced on the catapult would not cause any stick movement. Pilots were instructed to leave hands completely off the stick during the cat shot so that acceleration effects on the hand would not cause an unintended 'pull'. Any tendency to continue pitching nose up could be monitored primarily on an Airstream Direction Detector (ADD) gauge, which measured angle of attack. The need for keeping hands off the stick was shown during later night deck trials when one of our number left his hand on the stick unintentionally during a launch and left the catapult with almost full back stick on. The resulting nose-up pitch, noted via the ADD gauge, required immediate full forward stick to cancel.

Later in 1965 it was decided that a further Buccaneer Mk2 deck trial was required in tropical temperatures to confirm calculated performance. Choosing a site was a problem. Accommodation was required for a large engineering team ashore, with an RN aircraft carrier operating in tropical waters close at hand and with a programme that offered us sufficient time on the deck. Singapore or Aden seemed the only choices but local tensions in both places made the presence of an RN carrier unwelcome.

Of the other places considered, none met all the requirements, but the US Naval Air Station at Pensacola, Florida, met all but one and this shortcoming was met in a most agreeable way. No RN aircraft carrier was available in the Gulf of Mexico but the USN offered us the use of the carrier USS *Lexington* for five days! The *Lexington* was the current USN training carrier for its flying training base at Pensacola; the replacement for the USS *Monterey* on which I had done my first deck landings just ten years earlier in the SNJ.

Two Buccaneers left Boscombe Down in July and flew to Pensacola via Keflavik in Iceland, Goose Bay in Labrador and the US Navy Flight Test base at Patuxent River, Maryland. Unlike the Americans' own military aircraft, we did not have civil airways navigation equipment in the Buccaneers and so to conform with requirements we flew in company with a Boscombe Vulcan.

We went through a month of flying from the airfield at Pensacola, measuring fuel consumption and drag levels. The sort of temperature and humidity levels we had hoped for certainly presented themselves but on several days severe thunderstorms either ruled out flying completely or lowered temperatures to an impractical level. The Pensacola meteorological office lived up to the international reputation of met offices and provided a little light relief on one occasion. When asked if the thunderstorms they were predicting one day would be frequent, they replied, 'Well, some will be frequent and some will be infrequent.'

During the cockpit air-conditioning assessment phase of the trial, aircrews were weighed before and after each sortie to determine sweat loss. The most startling outcome of this check was not the weight lost during the flight, but the weight put on since the start of the trial. We had succumbed to that old American habit of eating, and who could blame us when even breakfast looked like a mess dinner.

The social side of the trial was as successful as the technical side and hospitality reached saturation point. The Americans were intrigued to see this unusually shaped aircraft on their base and queued up to be briefed on it. And I enjoyed revisiting the old haunts in Pensacola town, including the San Carlos Hotel of Horatio Nelson fame, unchanged over the ten-year gap.

For the deck trial aboard the USS *Lexington*, a third Buccaneer Mk2 joined us, flown in by Geoff Higgs and observer Tony Tayler. At our first meeting with the ship's executives, our chief performance engineer, Dennis Higton, outlined our catapult launching requirements, which included achieving a specific 'catapult end speed' relative to the ship. He asked if he could see the data that showed how much catapult steam pressure would give a particular end speed at various aircraft weights. The catapult officer shook his head and explained that here in the flying training command they had no such calibration. In their own training programme they just 'gave the catapult all the steam they'd got'. And so started a tense period of rethink as Dennis considered whether we should call off the proposed trials. It was vital to know to the nearest knot the speed at which the catapult would deliver the aircraft to the sky, or the planned data gathering could not begin.

After much discussion it was decided to start the trial with a session of calibration work. Four or five launches were made to draw up our own

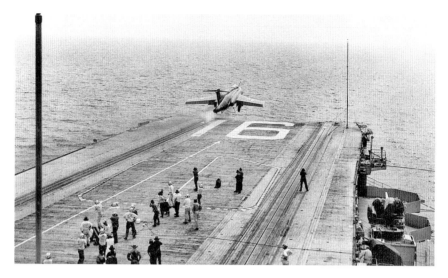

The first launch of a Buccaneer Mk2 during a deck trial on USS *Lexington* on 17 August 1965.

picture of the catapult characteristics before we began our trial to work on the objectives we had come for, namely to determine the limiting conditions for catapult launching at high weight and ambient temperature and to confirm adequate blow pressures at high ambient temperatures during twin- and single-engine approaches. Before the trial it had been estimated that the highest weight at which the minimum acceptable acceleration after catapult launch of 1½ knots per second, undercarriage down, could be achieved in temperatures of 30°C was 51,000lb. In fact, we went on in this temperature to 53,300lb and did not reach a limiting condition in either aircraft behaviour or acceleration.

We had set ourselves a limit of a 10ft drop off the catapult and this was certainly met when our heaviest and slowest launch was made, reserved of course for the CO, Geoff Higgs. A photograph was taken (see opposite) from the flight deck as Geoff went off the front at this condition and it shows just his aircraft's tailplane and nose clawing for the sky. But all the launches made confirmed the workability of the hands-off technique at the tailplane trim setting we used, though this area was to prove to be problematical when the first squadron went to sea the following year.

With observer Lt Ed Proctor, I flew the prototype '527 back to Boscombe Down, in company with our trusty Vulcan, via Patuxent River, Goose Bay

Buccaneer launch, 53,300lb. USS *Lexington*, 10ft drop.

A test briefing aboard USS *Lexington* in August 1965. Left to right: Author, Lt Chase, Cdr Higgs, Lt Cdr Tayler.

and Keflavik. As we had approached Iceland on our outward journey we had noted a column of smoke or steam coming up through the sea about 10 miles from the mainland. Now, as we approached Iceland on our return, we could see the same white column but it was now issuing from a small island that had developed there during the six weeks we had been away.

Cdr Geoff Higgs and observer Tony Tayler, with an extra fuel tank in their bomb bay, flew direct to RNAS Lossiemouth from Goose Bay, a trip of 2,000 miles in four hours twenty minutes, the first Atlantic crossing in one for a Fleet Air Arm aircraft.

At the beginning of the next year, 1966, I was given the trial of a new towed target system to be carried by the Sea Vixen and this gave us much amusement for several months. The target was designed to be used for anti-aircraft firing practice by ships at sea. The system consisted of a winch carried under the Sea Vixen's port wing containing a spool holding 20,000ft of piano wire, which could be reeled in or out by use of a four-bladed turbine mounted on the nose of the winch pod. On the end of the wire was a four-finned cylindrical target body, 8ft long and 8in in diameter, which could be fitted with radar reflectors, flares or miss-distance sensors to gauge how closely shells might pass. To bring the target back home after use it had to be reeled in and stowed on its launcher pad, also fitted under the port wing alongside the winch. Since capturing the target on its launcher was a tricky business, a periscope was fitted through the floor of the observer's cockpit to allow him to see the operation and fine-tune it during the final stages of recovery. My observer during these trials was 'Colonel' Kitchen, actually a lieutenant RN, and he had a control box from which he could launch, stream and supposedly recover the said target, by varying the blade angle on the turbine and the judicious use of an electrically operated brake.

From the cockpit I could see the nose of the target in its launcher, protruding forward of the left wing, and also the blades of the winch turbine. On our first streaming, when the target was made to drop away from the launcher only slowly, it was obviously affected badly by disturbed airflow when within about 3ft of the wing, and it swung violently from side to side. We increased the speed of the reeling out, but wondered how we were going to get it back in its box! It took some twenty minutes to stream the target to the full 20,000ft of its tow, at which time the target rode 1,500ft to 2,000ft below us depending on our speed. Winching in took a similar time.

Recovery of the target into its launcher was the fun part of the operation. The winch was set to wind in at maximum rate until there was 2,000ft to go and then slow down until, at about 150ft to go, the target appeared in the view of the periscope. It was then carefully wound in to a 'recovery position' approximately 3ft below the launcher and the brake applied. Winch blade angle was then increased to a stronger wind in level and then the observer simply waited until the oscillations of the target damped out completely, at which point he would select brake off and the target would leap into the launcher. If it managed to reach the launcher without succumbing to the effects of the air turbulence under the wing, it would lock in and we would breathe a sigh of relief. If, however, it started to swing there would be a flurry of the observer's hands towards the controls to reel the target out again before it beat itself to death against the wing and pylon. There was a touch of randomness about the behaviour of the target and the underside of our Vixen wing began to take on a beaten-up appearance. But eventually we were able to produce a set of instructions and a recommendation that the system be given clearance for fleet use.

In September 1966 we embarked for three days in HMS *Hermes* in the English Channel in the same pre-production Buccaneer Mk2 aircraft we had taken to the USA, this time to carry out night catapult launch and night deck landing trials. Again the trials were not expected to do anything other than confirm that the night clearance for the Mk1 Buccaneer could be read across to the Mk2, but here we extended the clearance to approach speeds at 5 knots below standard. Night deck landings are heavy breathing experiences no matter how much in practice you are. We took the precaution of taking four night catapult shots each on the shore-based catapult installed at the Naval Air Department at the Royal Aircraft Establishment Bedford before flying out to *Hermes*. And again, all our experience showed that the hands-off launch technique, using the proven tailplane trim settings, worked a treat.

At about the same time as our night deck trials, the navy's first Buccaneer Mk2 squadron, 801, was embarking in HMS *Victorious*. The ship was about to depart for the Far East but while still in home waters she announced the loss of a Buccaneer that had apparently pitched up and stalled after a hands-off catapult launch. The pilot was a newcomer to catapults and the suspicion was that he must have failed to follow the briefing and had his hand on the stick. However, shortly after *Victorious* began operating in the higher temperatures off Hong Kong, the squadron reported that all aircraft showed a tendency to pitch up off the catapult. They added they were briefing pilots carefully to be sure to have hands off, but what they did not reveal was that they were invariably pushing forward stick immediately after launch to counteract regular pitch-up behaviour.

Back at Boscombe, all the trials records were reviewed in an effort to understand the problem. All three pre-production aircraft had been used in deck trials to determine the correct trim setting so this was not suspected. The company design team came in with some new data, later revoked, that larger angle of attack (ADD) readings could be expected on launch in conditions of higher ambient temperatures due to an effect on the blow contribution to the wing lift coefficient. So in the end I was asked to go out to the ship and, armed with this knowledge, try to understand the cause of the problem. Having been involved in both day and night launch trials and the hands-off technique, I was as puzzled as the company designers as to the cause.

My brief was to carry out launches at the minimum launch speed, with the tailplane trim setting confirmed at minus 5.5 degrees (the setting arrived at after our trials) and to keep hands off and allow the aircraft to rotate off the catapult to 25 degrees ADD (1 degree higher than the normal squadron maximum allowed) before taking corrective action if necessary. I explained my brief to the squadron CO and to the squadron back-seater who had drawn the short straw to fly with me on the trial. Now the three pre-production aircraft we had used at Boscombe for our deck trials had had a scale painted on the fin against which the tailplane trim setting could be confirmed externally when the aircraft was on the catapult. I found that the squadron aircraft did not have the luxury of this external scale and so I decided to trust the cockpit trim gauge but to make the first launch at 5 knots above minimum launch speed instead of at minimum.

The trial was to be flown at the start of the day's operations and at 6.30 a.m. we lined up on the catapult. After the usual checks, I indicated all was well and the catapult officer signalled 'launch'. Immediately after the catapult fired, I concentrated on the ADD gauge and was confused to find that it didn't react at all but stayed at around zero (normally the gauge moved quickly during the launch to register approximately twenty as the aircraft left the ship). After about a second it moved up into the expected area above twenty but was moving at such a rate that it clearly wasn't going to stop at twenty-five. By twenty-four ADD I had full-forward stick on to try to control the pitch up but the aircraft continued to rotate nose up, stalled and dropped a wing, at which point I called for ejection and pulled the blind. The ship went hard starboard to avoid running over us and we were fished out of the sea by the plane guard helicopter.

The ejection itself was a blur. The aircraft was at about 90ft and 80 degrees of bank when we left, so the parachutes barely had time to open before we hit the sea. After a couple of days in the sick bay in *Victorious* I was transferred to the cruiser HMS *Tiger* and taken to the hospital at the Singapore naval base with strict instructions from the carrier's doctors to remain horizontal. I had three crushed vertebrae and the medical advice was not to stand or even sit upright. On arrival at the naval base the surgeon commander, who had not been told of my arrival and appeared to have no knowledge of ejection injuries, asked me to report to his surgery, felt around my damaged spine and pronounced that it was unlikely that I would be able to fly again. I explained that I had been told to stay horizontal but I was sent walking back to my accommodation. So I rang the senior doctor at the RAF Hospital Changi on the island and explained my situation. He told me to stay in bed until the RAF could collect me and I was taken over to the RAF hospital by ambulance, eventually to be casevaced back to the UK by Britannia transport aircraft. In the UK I spent a few days under observation in the RAF hospital at Wroughton, just a few miles from the Army Hospital in Tidworth, where my wife Raewyn was about to have our second child, Anna.

My RAF navigator, Flt Lt Colin Scriven, had no back problems initially but I believe he felt the effects later. My initial signal back to MoD Navy included:

Squadron pilots reveal that they do not, in any launch configuration, allow the aircraft to rotate naturally to a peak incidence, but rather they take the stick immediately after launch and … reduce the rotation. This … results in a complete lack of information on what 'natural' ADD peaks the squadron has been experiencing in any configuration and any over-trim effects will have been masked. Conclude temperature effects somehow further reduce stability, since pitch rate was so high.

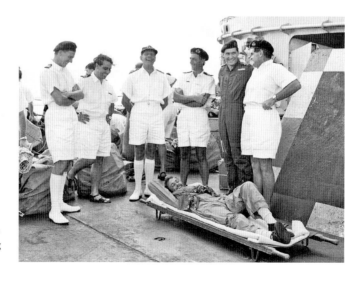

HMS *Victorious* in October 1966. The author is on a stretcher before his transfer to shore and return to UK following his ejection.

An investigation by Boscombe and the company then revealed that the trim gauging system in 801 Squadron's production aircraft had a different calibration to the one fitted in the three pre-production aircraft in which we had done our trials. Squadron aircraft using our recommendation were, in fact, all over-trimming by around 1 degree (setting our recommended -5.5 on the cockpit gauge gave -6.5 on the production standard aircraft), a significant error with the 'blown' tail. But the resulting pitch up would have been obvious, in time, to control it if the ADD gauge had functioned normally. I had experienced several interesting launch situations during trials, which had all been coped with (with reference to the ADD gauge). It was concluded that the ADD gauge had been faulty. And when the C Squadron CO visited the ship some months later to carry out some launches with the revised trim settings, he found a tool bag hanging from the ADD probe on an aircraft in the hangar! (The ADD probe is a delicate sensor that should be handled with great care to avoid damage.) In addition to a revision of the recommended tailplane trim settings to take account of the changed calibration, the company later redesigned the under-wing tank fairings to improve pitch stability at low speed, at the cost of some 2 per cent of high-altitude range.

Earlier in 1966, in the British government's defence review, it was announced that it had been decided to cancel the building of the new Royal Navy aircraft carrier, CVA-01, and to phase out the existing carriers. The loss of this major element of the defence force was to be balanced by 'a reduction in the UK's commitments', though the matching of political expectations against a budget to cover defence systems is a subject that rumbles on. When the rundown of the Fleet Air Arm was announced, and after some weeks of soul-searching, I decided to resign my commission and to seek to continue a test-flying career in industry. This decision did not come easily.

6

Buccaneer Front Line

In June 1966 I began enquiries about a civilian test-flying position with the major UK aircraft firms and with Grumman in the States. British Aircraft Corporation (BAC) at Warton in Lancashire had suffered a huge blow in 1965 when its TSR-2 project had been cancelled by the government, but Roland Beamont ('Bee') invited me for an interview and offered me a job as an experimental test pilot there. The normal routine when service test pilots were offered a post at a British company was for the RAF or the navy to allow the pilot concerned to join on a sixth-month trial period. After that time the pilot could either stay with the company or rejoin the service. In December 1966, while still recovering from my damaged spine, I applied to resign my commission to join BAC using that system. While the Admiralty was considering this request, my three-year appointment to Boscombe Down had been completed. After a month at the RAF Rehabilitation Unit at Headley Court nursing my back, I was sent to the navy's communications squadron, 781 at Lee-on-Solent, to fly Devon and Heron small passenger aircraft for three months of non-ejection seat flying. Having originally joined the navy as a short-service aviator and later been granted a permanent commission, I was now sent to sea on board the Dartmouth Training Squadron frigate, HMS *Scarborough*, for training to obtain a 'watch keeping ticket' and become a fully fledged 'fish-head'. I joined *Scarborough* in Plymouth in January 1967 but kept up the discussion on resignation with their lordships in parallel with my sea training. *Scarborough*'s captain, Cdr Tudor Craig, and first lieutenant, Lt Cdr John Carr, were somewhat startled to have a trainee in the rank of lieutenant commander but they provided a challenging programme.

The Admiralty eventually responded to my request to join the industry with the news that, owing to the loss in recent accidents of several Air Warfare Instructors (AWIs), I could not be spared and I would have to serve for a further two years. I was appointed initially as AWI of 809 Squadron (Buccaneers) in October 1967 and in January 1968 as senior pilot.

We embarked in HMS *Hermes* in November 1967, with the tailplane trim settings for catapult launch revised since my ejection just a year earlier. I remember being surprised to see how much more battered this working squadron's aircraft were compared to our three pre-production aircraft at Boscombe Down. *Hermes* sailed immediately to the South Atlantic for exercises and then past Cape Town and Durban and into the Gulf. We covered the British withdrawal from Aden before retiring to Masirah Island, Oman, for a barbeque Christmas dinner.

The Buccaneer had an excellent weapons system and we practised 2in rocketing and a low-level bombing technique of tracking the target with a depressed sight line, achieving an automatic bomb release triggered by a sensor monitoring the negative G build-up. The other interesting bombing method was toss bombing, both medium-range and long. The system was developed in the Buccaneer for delivery of the nuclear bomb in this Cold War environment. The aircraft radar and computers allowed us to assess a

A Buccaneer strike formation from HMS *Hermes* with 2in rocket pods.

potential ship target's course and speed from long range and at high altitude. Then the Buccaneer would slowly descend to sea level, staying below the target ship's radar horizon so that it could not be seen during the descent. Finally, we were to run in at high speed and very low level and deliver the bomb in a toss manoeuvre. We used to practise this exercise, throwing small 28lb practice bombs against a 'splash' target towed about 2,000ft behind the ship. Since the splash target was too small for the radar to lock on to it, the observer would lock on to the ship itself and feed into the computer a false target course and speed. This clever calculation would take into account the ship's actual course and speed, plus the length of the tow, the forecast wind and the time of flight of the bomb. This 'phantom' course and speed would, of course, be approximately 180 degrees out from the carrier's actual course. The pilot, tracking a marker in his attack sight, would be signalled to make a sharp pull up at the appropriate range, and the bomb would be released at about a 45-degree nose-up attitude. If this was war and you had just released a nuke you would now be keen to keep pulling until your heading was 180 degrees from the one you released on. But on these practice bomb runs you could instead roll over and more or less formate on your small bomb as it curved its way upwards and then down towards the small splash target well behind the ship. You could see the practice bomb splash down close to the towed target and it was always impressive to see the high accuracy we were achieving.

We were responsible to our masters to be able to guarantee a very high accuracy using 'real' bombs, and the difference between the ballistics of the small practice bomb and the 1,000 pounders were not truly tested in this context. So, armed with a good, consistent set of squadron results from our work on the *Hermes* splash target with the 28lb practice bomb, I went to see 'Wings', Cdr Stan Leonard. I explained that instead of throwing 28lb practice bombs at the splash target I would like to see how accurate we could be with inert 1,000lb bombs. He considered this request for several seconds and then his exact words were, 'F*** off!' So much for his trust in our clever calculation to fool the computer. The rival Buccaneer squadron in HMS *Eagle* practised just that technique later that same year.

In February 1968 we disembarked again to Lossiemouth and we were told that the Sea Vixen and Buccaneer squadrons from Hermes were to work up a formation aerobatic team for presentation at the Farnborough Air Show later that year. As the senior pilot of the Buccaneer squadron, 809, and therefore the leader of that team, I was enthusiastic to get started on such a pleasing task.

Phoenix Five aircrew (in black). Left to right: Dave Thompson, Robin Cox, Arthur White, Pete Sturt, Pete King, Author, Pete Mathews, Paddy Micklejohn, Dave Beddoe, Mike Cunningham.

The Buccaneer was not exactly an ideal aircraft for aerobatics but it would be fun to try to devise something new. Beneath it all, though, I was somewhat unhappy at the thought that the navy had delayed the start of my civilian career for two years, half of which was to be spent doing aerobatics.

The squadron was commanded by Lt Cdr Arthur White, an observer, whom I had known at Yeovilton as an observer instructor some nine years earlier. He was an excellent 'boss' with a good sense of humour. The squadron's primary aim was, of course, to stay in good strike-weaponry practice and so our aerobatic team work-up was tacked on to the end of our range firings and strike exercises.

Arthur and I discussed what display routine we might work on. The Buccaneer had a high wing loading, i.e. it was not a tight turning aircraft at the low to medium speeds we needed to hold in an aerobatic demonstration. What it did have, which was unique in a medium-sized aircraft, was a rotating bomb bay door. We decided to consider dropping balloons from our bomb bay, bearing the 'Fly Navy' message, over the crowd. The bomb bay was pretty voluminous and we reckoned we could fill the air for a short while if we filled all five aircraft. Since that would be a huge number of balloons and would involve some expense, we talked provisionally with the *Scottish Daily Mail* about some sponsorship, but we decided, wisely as it turned out, to have a dummy run to make sure that the balloons would exit in one piece. We loaded up the bay of one aircraft with thirty or forty inflated balloons, took off and, keeping the speed low, turned back over the field for the balloon drop. On opening the bomb door, thirty or forty pieces of rubber duly fell out and the idea was dropped. Instead we had 'Fly Navy' painted on the inside of the bomb doors of the display aircraft and opened them up during the slow flypast part of our routine.

We started practice with our team, now named the Phoenix Five (809 Squadron's crest was a phoenix) in March and at the beginning of September we flew it down to Yeovilton to practise co-ordinating our routine with the Vixen team, Simon's Sircus, led by my old friend Simon Idiens.

Simon's Sircus and Phoenix Five during 'anchor' formation at the Farnborough Air Show in 1968.

On one of our practice sorties at Yeovilton, I was told by our engineer officer that there had obviously been a gentle collision in the air between two of my team, since there was light wing-tip damage on two aircraft. The two pilots responsible claimed not to have noticed it but it had to be reported to higher authority, of course. I was given the inevitable roasting, but that was the last and only unhappy event. The Farnborough Air Show weather was good all week and, even without balloons, the show went well. The two teams appeared in 'anchor' formation on entry, then Simon pulled his Vixens up into a loop and we made a turn back to the centre of the airfield to start a series of alternating formation aerobatic manoeuvres that kept activity in front of the spectators throughout our seven minutes of 'on' time.

Back at Lossiemouth I continued with squadron armament practice until the middle of October, when I finally said goodbye to the Royal Navy after fifteen happy years. I was so much looking forward to work as a civilian test pilot that, surprisingly, my departure from the service, which had been my life since I left school, did not disturb my thoughts at the time as much as it has since. The navy had been my education in my formative years, in social as well as technical affairs. I loved its traditions and will be forever grateful for the opportunities it gave me.

7

Industry

I joined BAC at Warton in the middle of October 1968. Roland Beamont ('Bee') was the director of flight operations, Jimmy Dell was the chief test pilot and Tim Ferguson was his deputy. Bee had retired from test flying but remained as director nominally in charge of both flight operations and the flight test department. In fact, he took little active interest in the activities of the latter department except where it directly impinged on his pilots. Within a year after my arrival this anomaly had been noted and flight test was put under the control of the engineering director. Bee kept an eagle eye on all aspects of the flying at Warton and represented the interests of the aircrew as well as the current development status of the aircraft projects at the local board meetings. He had had an impressive war record with the RAF and had been chief test pilot for English Electric during its development of the Canberra, Lightning and TSR-2, carrying out the first flights of all three. The effect on his ego of this prodigious personal history was very evident and this earned him a mixed reputation.

Jimmy Dell was known by all as 'One of Nature's Gentlemen'. He, too, had had a star-studded career as a fighter pilot in the RAF, ending as a wing commander running the Air Fighting Development Squadron at West Raynham in 1959. When, later that year, Warton lost the services of two of their test pilots through illness, Jimmy was asked if he would be interested in leaving the RAF and joining the company. Once there, he played a major part in the development of the Lightning and in the early flying of TSR-2, which I had seen take to the air at Boscombe Down in 1964. When I arrived at Warton, Jimmy was the BAC project test pilot for the new Anglo-French Jaguar project and was spending a good deal of his time at Istres in France, where he was sharing the initial flying of the first prototype with Bernard Witt, chief test pilot of Sepecat/Breguet. Jimmy was an excellent boss and a real pleasure to work with.

Tim Ferguson, the deputy chief, ran the day-to-day flying programme and there were five other test pilots: Paul Millet, who had the title of senior experimental test pilot and like myself was ex-navy; John Cockburn; Peter Ginger and Reg Stock, who were experimental test pilots; and Eric Bucklow, production test pilot. In addition, Warton had four test navigators: Peter Moneypenny, the chief navigator; Jim Evans; Brian McCann and Ray Woollett. Roy Kenward was to join us from the navy in 1971.

At that time, the end of 1968, BAC had recovered from the tragedy of the cancellation of TSR-2 in 1965 and was busy with the Anglo-French Jaguar programme, with production testing and delivery of Lightnings and Strikemasters for Saudi Arabia, refurbishment and delivery of the Canberra for various South American air forces, and production testing and delivery of the final Jet Provosts for the RAF. Various minor programmes on in-service aircraft included the investigation into the cause of a couple of RAF incidents where the undercarriage of Lightning trainers had collapsed on landing. A two-seater had been assigned to look into this problem and it was a convenient time for me to get checked out again in the Lightning, having only flown it a couple of times at Boscombe Down. It was suspected that the hydraulic system plumbing on the two-seater was laid out in such a way that a heavyish landing could cause a ripple of pressure that could unlatch one of the down locks. For our investigation the undercarriage safety pins were left in place before take-off, the hydraulic system had instrumentation and a recorder fitted, and John Cockburn and I had the interesting brief to carry out some heavy touch-and-go landings. We were to attempt to achieve touch down descent rates of 10ft per second but in spite of my navy background of nil-roundout deck landings, we returned from three sorties unable to be so brutal. Meanwhile, parallel testing in the lab had found the cause so we were let off the hook of more attempts. The Lightning was an unforgettable aircraft to fly from the performance point of view and the new F.53s coming off the production line for Saudi Arabia were much looked forward to. A reheat take-off gave such a high acceleration that if the reheats were left lit after getting airborne, the landing gear had to be retracted sharpish to avoid exceeding the gear limiting speeds (see colour plate 20).

Another outstanding aspect of the design of the Lightning was the effectiveness and harmony of the flying controls throughout its wide speed range. From its 165 knots approach speed to its service limit of Mach 1.7, and apparently even to its experimental clearance to Mach 2 (although I didn't sample this higher speed), control was crisp, balanced and reasonably light, and with only moderate stick throw at all speeds. Bee had played a major part in perfecting this control harmony.

The final assembly of new Lightning aircraft was at Samlesbury, a BAC factory and airfield 15 miles east of Warton. Each first flight had to be flown out of there and landed at Warton after its first production test flight had been completed. The Samlesbury runway was only around 5,000ft long (Warton had 8,000ft) and once the brakes had been released on that first take-off you were virtually committed to getting airborne. Each new aircraft required an average of two to three further flights to complete the production test schedule and then the F.53s were readied for a one-hop delivery flight to Jeddah, in company with two or three others, using in-flight refuelling with RAF Victor tankers. These tankers could refuel three Lightnings simultaneously, the first plug-in being somewhere around Dover, the next over southern France and the final one over the Mediterranean short of Cairo. The flight from Warton to Jeddah took around six hours and in spite of the cramped fighter cockpit (we wore 'nappies') the mix of adrenalin produced by the three in-flight refuelling plugs and the breathtaking geography lesson unfolding across France, Italy, Crete, Egypt and Saudi, made these trips much sought after.

The in-flight refuelling task could be quite exciting, of course, if there was turbulence. I took the last of the two-seat Saudi Lightnings, the T.55, in September 1969, with Jimmy Dell in the right-hand seat, and on this one occasion we broke the journey at Akrotiri in Cyprus for the night. Having watched me plug in from the left-hand seat on the way in to Cyprus, Jimmy said he would like to try it from his position in the right-hand seat the following morning. With the refuelling probe being on the left wing this was likely to be somewhat more challenging. We met the tanker at 30,000ft or so but in heavy, clear air turbulence. Jimmy lost his enthusiasm for the exercise and it took me some five or six attempts to make contact. Once 'in' I elected to stay firmly attached for the duration of the final bracket.

On one delivery in April 1969, I was introduced to Saudi Arabian banking. We arrived in Jeddah on a Thursday afternoon and our small delivery team took a trip into the souk in the city. These delivery flights were usually led by ex-RAF Lightning pilot Dick Ingham, who after some mercenary time flying Lightnings for the Royal Saudi Air Force, had been invited to join the team at Warton for this type of exercise. Dick assured me we could change our traveller's cheques in one of the souk 'banks', which turned out to be a large shallow cupboard along the pavement, divided into pigeonholes about

6in sq., each holding an impressive roll of currency from one of thirty or forty countries. The obliging banker took our traveller's cheques for about £50 each, handed us each some riyal notes and coins and we headed off to eat. When we came to pay for our meal I discovered that my collection of Riyals consisted of only the minor notes and coins from the calculated exchange and I was missing the larger denomination notes. The souk was closed for the day and the following day was Friday, the Muslim Sabbath, when all was closed. We went back on the Saturday to the same impressive cupboard and found the individual who had dealt with us. I explained my predicament. He shrugged his shoulders. I asked if he didn't do an end-of-day stocktake at each close of play and again he shrugged. Dick, who had lived in Saudi Arabia for a couple of years, stepped forward and said something to the effect of, 'Look, this is an honourable Englishman who is saying that you made a mistake.' The banker looked at us both for a moment, then slowly reached for his roll of Riyals and counted out the missing funds. I was impressed.

During my last months in the navy, the Ministries of Defence of several European countries were struggling with decisions on re-equipping their strike fleets for the continuing Cold War. In Britain, cancellation of the TSR-2 in 1965 had led to consideration of acquiring the American F-111, while continuing to study development of an Anglo-French variable geometry, small strike aircraft. The French pulled out of this idea in 1967 and BAC continued with its own swing-wing studies. The British government felt that a European collaborative project would be the way to go and discussed common requirements with a group of European nations looking to replace their F-104s. These nations included West Germany, Italy, Belgium and Holland, but the latter two left the discussions in 1967/68. In 1969, the UK, West Germany and Italy agreed to go ahead with the Multi-Role Combat Aircraft (MRCA) development and in 1969, the Panavia Company was set up in Munich, comprising personnel from the three companies, British Aircraft Corporation, Messerschmitt-Bölkow-Blohm and Fiat, later Aeritalia. Panavia was to co-ordinate the activities of those three partner companies from its headquarters in Munich. The UK, West Germany and Italy initially committed to purchase, respectively, 385, 600 and 200 MRCAs, though these numbers reduced somewhat as the project went along.

In flight operations at Warton I was tasked by Jimmy Dell in 1970 to look after this embryonic project and with Ricky Richardson, the company's military liaison officer, I began to visit Panavia in Munich on roughly a monthly basis (Ricky was an ex-Battle of Britain Spitfire pilot and on one of our first visits I saw him physically bristle when a German shouted 'Achtung' to attract our attention as we walked away from a meeting). The three companies were responsible for particular parts of the aircraft system design and construction and since BAC was to build the nose section, we became responsible for the co-ordination of the cockpit design. With the title of BAC MRCA project pilot, I started then, in 1970, to propose the cockpit layout for the proposed NATO strike fighter. I worked with two design engineers from the Warton drawing office, Arthur Lowe and Bob Rigg, and together we drew up a multitude of presentations and various cockpit mock-ups in wood and eventually metal. A monthly 'CCCC' meeting was instituted, the Cockpit Co-ordination and Control Committee, at which the project pilots from the three companies plus pilot representatives from the three defence ministries, discussed our proposals.

A very early VVIP visitor to the MRCA mock-up was His Royal Highness the Duke of Edinburgh. He was highly amused that I was the project pilot of 'just a wooden mock-up' but on showing him around the cockpit he took a keen interest in all the detail. He wanted to know how the guns were fired and I showed him the trigger stowed on the stick top that could be flicked into a firing position. But our simple mock-up version allowed access on the stick top to the firing microswitch within the stick, without the need for the trigger to be unhoused. He quickly latched on to this and took great pleasure in pointing it out!

The UK and West Germany, by virtue of their latest declared planned purchase numbers, were each assigned 42.5 per cent of the design and build work and Italy claimed the other 15 per cent. Initially the cockpit meetings were held monthly alternating between Munich and Warton, and each lasted three days. The agendas were long and argumentative and the time in the meeting room was maximised by having a 'working lunch', i.e. plates of sandwiches and coffee or lemonade were devoured while continuing the discussions. The format was along the lines of BAC presenting a proposed layout or diagram of a specific instrument or control panel, specialists from the design office then being paraded to back up technical questions, and the representatives from the air forces (i.e. the customer) discussing what had been proposed.

Of course, during the cockpit definition activities flying at Warton continued. Jimmy Dell and Paul Millett were heavily involved with Jaguar, both at Warton and in Toulouse. Tim Ferguson, John Cockburn, Peter Ginger,

HRH Prince Philip inspects the early MRCA mock-up at Warton in June 1972.

The Phantom F-4K had two Rolls-Royce Spey engines with reheat.

Reg Stock and Eric Bucklow kept the Warton programme going, with production flying of the Lightning F.53s coming off the production line for Saudi Arabia, Strikemasters also for Saudi, Canberra rebuilds for Venezuela, Ecuador and Peru, and various programmes of changes to the RAF fleet. Although the MRCA work was intensive and absorbing I was able to keep current in flying on these various programmes. I also had a stroke of luck by being in Jim Dell's office one day in March 1971 when he had a phone call from Cliff Rogers, chief test pilot of Rolls-Royce at Hucknall. Rolls had persuaded the MoD to fit the reheated Spey engine into the UK Phantom fleet, the F-4K and F-4M. The first Phantom F-4Ks had been delivered to

Hucknall and they needed some pilot help to build up some flying data quickly. Jim looked at me and said, 'Well I think I have someone right here who could help!'

One of several reasons that I was sad to leave the Fleet Air Arm three years earlier was that I would lose the opportunity of flying the Phantom, which had just been ordered for the service. I went down to Hucknall in April and May that year and had a brief taste of it, just ten hours. I flew first with Graham Andrews, one of the four Rolls-Royce test pilots, and then with a flight test engineer, gathering performance data at altitude. I was very impressed with the roomy cockpit layout and the well-organised cockpit procedures.

I was somewhat surprised to find the handling was on the heavy side, certainly compared with the Lightning, and in the circuit needed rudder to co-ordinate roll, in spite of having spoiler control rather than ailerons. Being well liked in the US Navy as a deck landing aircraft, this behaviour was not expected.

Hucknall was very busy at that time with much activity on the large civil engine side and an impressive line-up of flying test beds. And in the corner of a hangar was a Spitfire Mk.XIV that Cliff generously offered me a trip in as a thank you for helping them out (as if I needed a thank you). Sadly, at the end of the Phantom data gathering, the Spitfire was having a major overhaul, but I was assured that I would be welcome back to Hucknall when it was back in one piece, and I didn't allow Cliff to forget!

Back at Warton, I was privately pretty unhappy not to be involved in the early Jaguar development. This shiny, new supersonic aircraft with a first generation inertial navigation and attack system and new reheated Adour engines seemed to be doing exciting things while I was attending MRCA meetings and assessing mock-ups. The Jaguar had made its first flight in France a month before I joined the company in October 1968 but I didn't get into it until February 1971. The early UK flying was done by the chief and deputy chief test pilots, Jimmy Dell and Tim Ferguson, and by Paul Millet, who succeeded Jimmy as chief test pilot when Jim sadly failed his medical in late 1970.

In September 1971, with the MRCA in early build and much activity in the design office working on the avionics systems, we took delivery from the navy of the first of two Buccaneer Mk2 aircraft that were to be modified to take the MRCA navigation and weapons system for development prior to the appearance of MRCA itself. One of our navigators, Roy Kenward, was

John Cockburn and the author with the outstanding Warton support staff during production testing of the 99th and 100th Warton Jaguars.

himself ex-navy and familiar with the Buccaneer so he and I went across to the Naval Air Station at Eglinton, Northern Ireland, and collected Buccaneer XT272, taking it to West Freugh where we checked it out with four sorties to confirm that it met the standard performance schedule. We found that it had a chequered history, having suffered a heavy landing at Lossiemouth, during which the observer had ejected! It was no wonder that this was an aircraft the navy was keen to give away to our programme, since it was carrying something of a twist and above 550 knots the aircraft built up an increasing amount of yaw. However, we concluded that this was not going to influence the sort of trials we had planned for it so we noted the problem and on 16 September 1971 delivered it to Cambridge, where the Marshalls Company was to remove its nose section and graft on the planned MRCA bulbous nose, housing its two radar antennae and major parts of the planned weapons and navigation systems.

Also in late 1971, we progressed to an accurately detailed mock-up of the MRCA cockpits, which were quite roomy. The stick top and all cockpit panels were modelled accurately with appropriate switchery and in some cases we were able to get hold of the actual intended instruments. Roland Beamont, now director of flight operations for Panavia, floated the idea that the head-up display symbology should be projected straight on to the windscreen, an arrangement he had championed in his wartime Tempest squadron days. We looked at this but found that there were many complications, not least the expected distortion of the windscreen caused by air pressure at high speed.

We also ran an investigation into the relative merits of analogue versus digital instrumentation. The Dutch had produced an excellent paper on the subject. We found that Concorde was using engine instruments that combined both; a conventional analogue, round dial showing, for instance, engine revs, with an accurate digital readout in the centre of the same gauge. To the delight of the programme manager, we adopted these gauges, which were 'off the shelf'. Having arrived at the number of separate cockpit panels that were required on the side consoles, there were several weeks of discussion on relative importance of the 'reachability' of those panels and in what order they should be placed. This involved exercises simulating an operational sortie, checking required hand movements at the various stages of an attack profile.

The cockpit (CCCC) meetings were initially held alternatively at Warton and Munich. After the early ones, the Italian project pilot, Peter Trevisan, asked that Aeritalia should also be allowed to host some of these monthly meetings at its base in Turin. This was duly set up in February 1972 and we met in the splendid oval-tabled boardroom at the old Fiat Aviazione headquarters building in Caselle. As explained earlier, these cockpit meetings had a huge agenda to get through each month and took three days. When lunchtime arrived on the first meeting at Caselle, instead of a sandwich and coffee snack being offered, through which we could keep on working, we were herded on to a bus and taken down town to an upmarket restaurant. In spite of our objections and calls for minimum time away, we waded through a wonderful spread including wines, of course, and got back to work some three hours later. I asked Peter to arrange for a working lunch in the meeting room the following day but the next morning he explained that company rules would not allow that, but he would endeavour to have a shorter meal at the restaurant. That day and the final day, lunch still took some two hours and we left Caselle with around half of the agenda untouched. The cockpit meeting schedule reverted again to just Warton and Munich. However, after about a year Peter called and said that he had finally got agreement for a working lunch to be allowed in the Fiat boardroom and could we get back to including Turin in the meeting round. A Turin meeting was arranged and at lunchtime the great doors of the boardroom were opened and in marched five or six suitably uniformed waiters pushing steaming trolleys. The papers scattered about were pushed aside and neat sets of knives, forks, spoons, glasses and plates were introduced, followed by another superb lunch! It was a further six months before Aeritalia finally lowered its catering standards to those of the other two partner companies.

Before each meeting of the CCCC I would prepare, in conjunction with the Warton design office, diagrams of the proposed console panel or instrument, and discuss these with our own RAF project aircrew. This would give us a strong UK party line prior to discussion at the full international meeting, where we were liable to meet extraordinary proposals. I remember that MBB at one of the early meetings proposed not one but three small switches to raise the landing gear, one for each wheel! This was the brainchild of a Dr Seifert, an amusing but remote psychiatrist acting as MBB's cockpit design advisor. It was sometimes a good discipline though, to have challenged views that needed to be thought back to first principles rather than simply tabled because that was the way it had always been done.

One requirement that was emphasised heavily by the project directors was 'commonality'. We were told in no uncertain terms that to keep costs down the four air forces involved, West German Air Force, West German Navy, Italian Air Force and RAF, *must* have common cockpit items. The intention was to be able to order 800 of each and every item, not 300 altimeters of that type for the RAF and different altimeter types again for the other customers (the German and Italian military aircraft were mainly of American design and they were used to different cockpit instrument presentations). At one meeting at Warton I presented the proposed layout for the environment control system panel. A switch on that panel had an engraved marking 'A.V.S.' to control flow to the aircrew air-ventilated suit. Although this garment was proposed to keep the aircrew cool in hot climates, the Italians, who dwelt in the potentially hottest country of the three initial customers, had decided not to fit this system. The panel I proposed was for all three customers but I showed that a small blanking plate was to be used in the Italian aircraft to cover up the hole and the engraving provided for the A.V.S. switch for the other two countries. The major from the Ministry of Defence in Rome said there was no way he was going to approve a panel with a hole it didn't need; Italy would have a panel with no covered-up switch hole. I gave my plea for commonality. He was unmoved. In turn, German and British MoD officials tried their powers of persuasion for commonality. Eventually an old friend from my ETPS course, Wg Cdr Ned Frith, representing MoD London, said, 'Look, when God made men and women, he gave them both nipples. The men don't use theirs; they're just there for commonality.' There was a moment's reconsideration and then the good major agreed.

The UK Ministry of Defence Procurement Executive required that the industry's test pilots involved in MoD contracts should maintain a minimum flying currency level of fifteen hours a month. This could be flown on current test-flying programmes or on the company's executive aircraft; we had an Aztec, a Cessna 420 and a ten-seat, twin jet, HS.125. Once the MRCA programme got going, the company established a regular passenger service to Munich and to Turin with the HS.125 to take engineers to the inevitable and seemingly endless meetings. Ray Woollet (Ray was by now our chief navigator and the MRCA project navigator) and I used to pilot this service whenever we had meetings to attend there such as the CCCC. On one occasion,

Tornado cockpit mock-up at Warton in 1974.

sharing the Munich HS.125 trip with Reg Stock, our chief executive flight pilot, I was navigating on the return leg to Warton when I gave our position report as we entered a new air traffic sector, quite late at night. Something like, 'Romeo Foxtrot, Frankfurt at 05, Flight Level 385, estimating Hamm at 20.' The German controller came back with, 'What is your estimate for X?' Unused to a sense of humour in this part of the world we were astonished when we queried 'X' to be told, 'You give me ETA for Ham, I ask you ETA for X, Ham and X. This is a joke!' Well, at least he was trying.

This flying time contributed to the MoD monthly requirement, as did a sharing out of the Lightning and Strikemaster production flying and the deliveries of Lightnings, Strikemasters and Canberras. These deliveries were the highlights of the flying programme in those days and the sharing was observed meticulously. The Canberra deliveries to Venezuela, Ecuador and Peru were planned expertly by the navigators. In the winter we took the southern route, down through Rabat, crossing the Atlantic from Dakar in Senegal, or from Monrovia, Liberia, to Recife, Brazil, a four-hour thirty-minute trip. Then, we flew around the South American coast, through Surinam, Maracay in Venezuela, Chiclayo in northern Peru and on to Lima. In the summer, when the Canadian snows had cleared, we used the northern route through Goose Bay in Labrador or Halifax in Nova Scotia, and on down to South America through either Bermuda or Baltimore and the Bahamas. The Canberra had cartridge starters for its Avon engines. The cartridge was inserted into the starter through the spinner on the engine's nose and at the various stops in South America there was usually a queue of locals waiting to collect the spent cartridge case that we discarded when we loaded a new one before each start. The cases were copper and approximately 10in long and 3in in diameter, so they were pretty attractive and a good bargaining tool.

The Canberra itself was a pretty uncomfortable aircraft in heat or turbulence. In the tropics, just strapping in and going through the checks under its burning glass style of cockpit canopy left you pretty exhausted and dehydrated. There was no ground cooling, just a small, 6in diameter, circular, hinged, direct-vision panel in the canopy that could be opened on the ground, or in flight for landing if iced up. The RAF had a rule for tropical operation that, once strapped in, if you weren't airborne in fifteen minutes, you must shut down, leave the cockpit and cool off. The navigator in the B2 version sat at a table behind the pilot's rear bulkhead and on it he had a small fan that could direct a cooling flow at his face. On one delivery with navigator Jim Evans we had taken off from the Bahamas and were just settling into the climb en route for Maracay, Venezuela, when there was a significant thud followed by a low frequency vibration. I checked the engine instruments for clues. No apparent problems. The steady vibration was discernible through the cockpit structure and I began to reason that an external panel must have come adrift. Would it be wise to continue? Just then Jim called that he had found the cause. One of the rubber blades had come off his desk fan!

It was on a similar delivery, this time via Bermuda to Peru and also with navigator Jim Evans, that we carried a horseradish plant as a gift for our company rep in Lima. On our previous delivery he had invited us to dinner at his home in the Lima suburbs and his attractive Peruvian wife had cooked a superb meal of roast beef. He apologised for the lack of horseradish sauce, saying that it wasn't obtainable in Peru and although he brought loads back on his yearly trips back to the UK it never quite kept up with their consumption. I offered to bring him some rootstock that an old family friend, Leslie Milnes, provided from his Kirklees garden, and we carried this large, ugly, white root plus a few handfuls of soil wrapped in transparent plastic on the floor of the navigator's cockpit. We had been warned to moisten the soil at each stop but on arriving in Bermuda on a Friday afternoon, and no doubt being keen to get to the hotel, we had closed the door on 'the root' without remembering to give it a drink. It was while taxiing out on Monday morning that Jim noticed our parcel and reported that it now looked pretty shrivelled up. During the climb up to our cruising height, Jim announced that he had had a generous idea and donated to the root the contents of his bladder. On arrival in Lima our gift was handed over but without full disclosure of its adventures. That was my last trip to Lima and I guess I will never know how successful Jim's first-aid treatment was.

It was on one return from a Canberra delivery that I managed to include a Concorde trip. Our return tickets from these exploits were always first class with BOAC and on this occasion the flight was via New York. On the check-in desk was a notice advertising the possibility of an upgrade to Concorde for £50. I couldn't resist and got more flight time at Mach 2 plus during that return than during the rest of my test-flying career! Paul Millet and I had an invitation from Brian Trubshaw during the development phase of Concorde to visit him at Fairford and join him on a test flight. Paul had managed to fit this in and had been allowed a few minutes' handling, but I couldn't spare the time to join him at that time and sadly the opportunity passed.

When I had left the navy at Lossiemouth in October 1968, Raewyn and I were keen to find a house we could refurbish in the countryside around

Warton. The Fylde area itself is pretty flat and windswept and so we looked further east along the Ribble Valley. Eventually we bought Gatecote Farm, a rundown farmhouse and barn alongside the River Darwen at Samlesbury. For our first five or six years with BAC we put every spare penny into refurbishing this gem of a homestead. We had 1.5 acres and I re-established my beekeeping interests there, building up to ten hives. Raewyn took up supply teaching as our own two children started school.

Prior to the start of the MRCA flying programme, each of the partner companies developed their own simulator so that aircrew could get some familiarity with the likely flying characteristics. Initially all three were significantly different even though they were supposedly using the same data. But as time went on they drew closer together in their 'feel'. Unlike my later experience with simulation prior to first flight of the EAP, the early simulation of MRCA was not particularly helpful to the pilots, though an important part of the development, of course, for the engineers.

During 1973 the Jaguar development programme increased in intensity and I began to get more development flying in this interesting aircraft. Being

The author with his bees at Gatecote Farm in the summer of 1973.

destined for use as a ground-attack aircraft it was to be cleared to carry a long list of under-wing and under-fuselage stores and much of the work was to check and clear the handling with various weapons, both symmetrical and asymmetrical. The task was usually to carry out endless wind-up turns, achieving simultaneously a required specific airspeed (or Mach number), altitude, G and roll rate, looking for handling difficulties such as pitch up, heavy stick forces, buffet or lumpy roll response. Also, the first Jaguars were beginning to come off the production line and so in addition to the endless MRCA cockpit meetings and rig checks, I was getting back to a reasonable amount of test flying too.

In addition to the Buccaneer hack aircraft, the MRCA programme included a 'hack' to carry the MRCA engine for development before the aircraft itself was due to get airborne. The last Vulcan B.1 in UK service was modified to carry it in a pod below the belly, shaped like a section of the MRCA fuselage and engine air intake. This pod would also contain a Mauser 27mm cannon to allow investigation of the effects of gun gas ingestion into the engine. The go-ahead for the engine had been delayed by the procurement system until some six months after the agreement to build the MRCA itself, and so it was hoped that by getting the engine airborne underneath the Vulcan, engine development would be well advanced by the time of the MRCA's first flight. Rolls-Royce test pilot John Pollitt began the Vulcan test bed flying from the company airfield at Hucknall in April 1973 and Paul Millett and I were later invited to fly with him. Experience on the flying test bed was certainly hugely helpful but unfortunately the full 350 hours planned was not achieved after the Vulcan itself became unserviceable with structural and electrical problems.

As already mentioned, the three Tornado main contractor companies, in addition to having defined shares of the aircraft manufacture, also had defined responsibilities for the various systems. BAC had responsibility for the hydraulic system and so we had the complete hydraulic rig laid out in a hangar, capable of functioning a set of spoilers, tailplane, wing sweep and landing gear, selectable from a mocked-up cockpit. The hydraulics engineers used the rig for testing and at the cockpit end we were able to confirm satisfactory selectors and indicators. It was here we found that the rudder trim selector, a rotary knob under the cockpit left coaming, could be turned to give full rudder trim deflection, say left, but a tweak more in the left direction made the rudder spring to full right! The selector signalling on the first experimental panel was imprecise. Aeritalia, responsible for the fuel

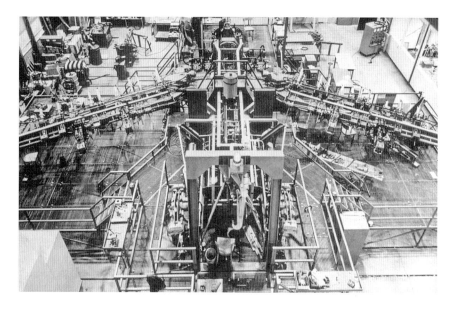

MRCA hydraulic rig at Warton in 1974.

system, had a similarly representative fuel rig in Turin, where the tanks could be made to invert to simulate negative G and confirm correct flow. The flying control rig was in Munich since the Germans had the responsibility for the Control and Stability Augmentation System (CSAS). The test aircrew from all three contractors visited each other's rigs, mock-ups and simulators to discuss experience in them and to gain familiarity.

One cockpit control that was new to all of us was the wing sweep lever. It was inevitably going to be an agricultural looking lever inboard of the throttles but the sense of operation was the subject of debate. Should it be forward to move the wings forward, or, like the throttles next door, forward to go faster i.e. to sweep the wings back? After airing it in house we agreed 'forward to sweep the wing forward' and we were gratified when Paul and I went down to the USAF base at Upper Heyford to fly the F-111 simulator and discussed the subject there. We found that Grumman, which worked with General Dynamics on the design, had initially designed its lever to work in the other sense but that after criticism it was changed around at considerable expense.

In July 1974, as the first prototype MRCA was approaching its first flight in Germany, Roy Kenward and I had a very enjoyable short detachment to

Bedford where the first of the two Buccaneer hack aircraft, XT272, was to be flight-tested with its new nose and avionics. A Marshalls engineering team from Cambridge, led by its chief engineer, Peter Bensted, had prepared it for a series of tests to confirm its handling with the slightly changed aerodynamics and centre of gravity. In order to avoid Marshalls becoming liable for a financial penalty if it was delivered late, we persuaded Bedford airfield to remain open late on the evening of the last day of the contract to allow us to get in the final check flight and deliver it to Warton.

John Cockburn, who had done much of the navigation system development on the Jaguar, became our specialist on the Buccaneer avionics test bed and he and I picked up the second Buccaneer hack after conversion at Cambridge and flew it into Bedford in October 1974. But the introduction of these two flying test beds into the development programme was, like the Vulcan, somewhat late. Both would have shortened development time if they could have been available six months earlier.

When the MRCA programme contracts were signed back in 1969, it was agreed that the first flight would be in Germany with a British pilot and that the second and third prototypes would fly from Britain. Paul Millet, the Warton chief test pilot, went over to Manching in April 1974 to prepare for the flight and to carry out engine runs and system checks. Manching was

Marshall's engineering team with modified Buccaneer XT272 at Bedford in July 1974. The author is sixth from the left, Peter Benstead is seventh from left and Roy Kenward is tenth from the left.

West Germany's government military aircraft test base, about 100km north of Munich, and MBB shared the facility. During an engine run just prior to the planned first flight, the left engine failed with an impressive bang and Paul returned to the UK until the problems had been sorted out. Eventually, modified engines were ready and Paul flew the first flight with Nils Meister, the MBB MRCA project pilot, in the rear seat on 14 August 1974. The flight was completely successful and the flying programme was finally under way. Meetings of the CCCC continued, since the production standard of the cockpit was still not defined completely, and Paul flew the first flight of our British prototype, P02, at Warton three months later. On this first flight of our first British prototype, I was hoping that I would at least be in the back seat with Paul but because this was a three-nation programme it was decided – and rightly – that we should fly the Italian project test pilot, Pietro Trevisan, in the back and I had to satisfy myself with flying the Canberra chase plane.

The RB199 engine was still giving trouble when the test programme started. Paul and I had done endless engine runs in P02 on the engine running bay on the south side of Warton airfield. The experience made us very familiar with the cockpit and with the various warnings that the early engines threw up. On the day of P02's first flight I took off early in the Canberra and flew circuits over the runway as Paul taxied out. He lined up, went through his checks and I positioned myself overhead to pick him up as he got airborne. He ran up to maximum dry thrust and as I ran in expecting him to release the brakes, I saw a flash of flame in the left engine jet pipe, indicating a significant engine surge. He throttled both back to idle and began to discuss the problem with 'Boffin', our online telemetry engineer, Dave Williams. Paul said that the engines had looked fine from the cockpit indications and asked what had been picked up from the telemetry. After the usual delay, Boffin reported that they could see nothing wrong and that it was 'up to Paul if he went or not'! Paul went, of course, and we had a very successful first flight of P02.

The early engines, we soon learned, were liable to surge if they were run up quickly from cold to max. We instituted the 'Elephant Procedure'★, which

★ The elephant procedure is so called because early explorers in India had allegedly been advised to leave a fire burning in the bush overnight to dissuade the elephants from trampling their tents. The trampling stopped but no one knew if it was the fire that had done the trick.

consisted of running up to max dry for five seconds, then throttling to idle and finally back to max and on into take-off. Rolls-Royce eventually ran an engine in a test bed while X-raying it and determined that with initial uneven heating up of the various modules, the close tolerances caused the rotating blades to make interference contact with other parts, distorting the airflow and leading to a compressor stall.

I eventually got to fly the object that had occupied me for the previous five years when I took our first prototype for its second flight on 18 November 1984. It is, of course, impossible to describe the unique feelings generated by such an experience. It was a strange combination of total familiarity with the machine from an engineering standpoint, and of the cockpit, but a clean sheet of paper with regard to its airborne behaviour and an enormous thrill that it was finally happening. Memories of my earliest impressions of that first flight are primarily that I found the aircraft handling – its response to control inputs – was totally conventional. I was expecting that the effects of the fly-by-wire 'manoeuvre demand' system would feel somewhat unusual. In all the previous aircraft I had flown, a particular stick input in pitch gave a specific change of tailplane (or elevator) angle, and that new tailplane angle would give a particular pitch rate depending on your airspeed. With MRCA's manoeuvre demand system, that same particular stick input is interpreted as a demand for as much tailplane movement as is necessary to achieve a particular pitch rate, regardless of airspeed.

On this first experiencing of the system I was surprised – and impressed – that this significant change in the control system could not be detected readily. It is this feature that makes the Tornado handling feel unchanged no matter what you load it up with and no matter at what speed you are flying (see colour plate 21).

Paul Millett and I flew together alternately in the front or the back seat of P02 for the first twenty or thirty flights. The back seat had no flying controls but carried some instrumentation and a more comprehensive warning panel than the front. It was on flight eighteen on 2 April 1975 that we came close to losing it. Paul was in the front seat and we had a schedule that required us to look at the aircraft's power off-take capability at high altitude and then to make some airspeed indicator checks by flying past the Warton tower at various pre-arranged airspeeds for cine camera recording of actual speed. To check power off-take performance we were to arrange engine settings to give each engine, individually and in turn, the load from the gearbox while sweeping the wing to achieve maximum hydraulic load. The early engines

Paul Millett (left) and the author with MRCA prototype P02 in February 1975.

had problems carrying this load individually and we were to investigate limits at high altitude where the engine was closest to its surge boundary. After several load checks, the left engine surged impressively and over-temperatured during a sweep at low speed. The Turbine Blade Temperature (TBT) warning gave us a blast and we had exceeded the declared limit by 50 degrees or so. This was serious enough to go back home gently to look for damage and Paul simply left that engine idling, since it showed no further signs of distress. Back at base we decided to do a couple of airspeed checks past the tower using just the good engine and on one run, stabilised at the lowish airspeed of 190 knots, we swallowed a seagull down the right (good) engine intake. There was an impressive bang accompanied by a right engine TBT warning and I could see in the mirror that we were towing a tongue of flame. Paul slammed both engines to max reheat but the right engine fire warning lit so he shut it down. We were now relying on the left engine we had over-temperatured at height.

As Paul cleaned the aircraft up – we had lowered flap and gear for the airspeed check run – it became clear that in spite of the reheat selection we were losing height and speed. But, for the first time, the reheat had failed to light, although the reheat nozzle had opened up so we were getting somewhat less-than-even maximum dry thrust. We headed for an open space and contemplated ejection. Then suddenly, the engine surged, as was to be expected with a nozzle wide open and reheat unlit. Instinctively Paul pulled the throttle back to dry power, the nozzle closed and we could feel the thrust increase. We had come down to about 300ft over the marshland to the east of Warton airfield and we turned back and climbed up to circuit height, breathing again.

P02, as our first prototype, had non-standard intakes with a small pitot sensor fitted inside for data gathering. The bird had collected this item and fed it into the fan, so mashing up the first stage even more impressively than would otherwise have been the case.

Initial progress with the test programme was slow. Never develop a new airframe with a new engine. Problems with the one delays progress with the other. However, in August 1975 I made the first flight in our second airplane, P03. This was our first trainer, so had a full set of flying controls in the back cockpit. Tim Ferguson, who at that time was Warton's deputy chief test pilot, flew in the back on flight one and sampled some handling from the rear seat. Over the next ten days we flew twelve flights in the trainer and at last we began to see some shape in the development programme. During this first look at the two-seater we flew Bee, now director flight operations Panavia, in the rear seat, for an early look and also one of the MBB project pilots, Ahmin Krauthann, who was still to fly the German prototype.

It was later this year that we were able to sample for the first time the performance of the terrain-following radar (TFR) that was now fitted and

Right engine damage on P02 flight eighteen on 2 April 1975.

operating in our hack Buccaneer, XT285. In the hack the system was wired up to the flight director only, not to the Buccaneer autopilot, but we were able to begin gathering data during low-flying sorties over the Lake District and southern Scotland. One of the TFR targets we used was the sheer-sided Ailsa Craig island, due west of Girvan and south-west of Prestwick in the Irish Sea. Running at this island at low level and waiting for the command to pull up obtained your full attention.

In December 1975 I made the first flight in P06, the sixth (Warton's third) MRCA, now christened Tornado. This was to be our Mauser cannon test aircraft and so the ammunition bays, which on the earlier prototypes had been full of flight test instrumentation, had to be available for proper use. The flight test instrumentation recording gear was therefore moved to the rear cockpit and so the aircraft always had to be flown solo. P06 was a very serviceable aircraft from the beginning and the pace of our data gathering now began to build up strongly. P06 was to introduce slight changes to the rear end geometry below the fin to improve directional stability by adding to the profile of the reverser buckets and so effectively extend the lower fin area when the buckets were closed. Our early experience with P02 and P03 had shown that the aircraft had excellent directional stability and gave a very smooth ride in all wing sweeps and throughout the speed range. But when the revised reverser bucket shapes were flown for the first time on P06, directional stability was reduced and the changed profile brought with it a light but annoying rear fuselage buffet. This latter became a feature at a specific speed/Mach number combination of roughly 350 knots at 10,000ft. The intensity varied slightly for no apparent reason and in the early part of 1976 we flew many hours in P06 and in P02 experimenting with subtle lower fin profile changes to try to eliminate these two changes. We established a scale of buffet intensity that we plotted on a Mach number/indicated airspeed/altitude carpet as the engineers modified a wooden lower fin profile with a spoke shave between flights. The project director, Garry Willox, was somewhat unhappy at our using up flight time to try to reach a profile giving totally smooth flight but we ended up with a much-improved situation. It was while this exercise was going on that I flew the F-104 Starfighter at MBB in Manching and took on a wholly new view of what buffet levels were acceptable! The F-104 was quite smooth above Mach 1 but at subsonic speeds it sat in permanent 'cobblestones'!

The thrust reverser itself had been specified in order to meet the tight specifications for stop distances demanded by the defence ministries.

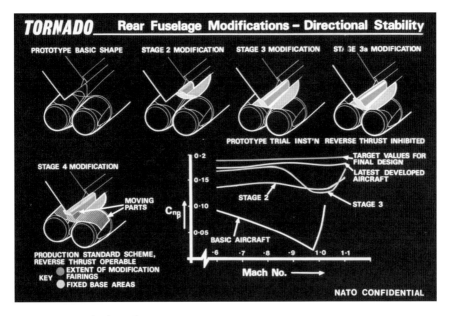

Progressive rear fuselage changes.

They had an eye on the use of short stretches of motorway during possible operations on the European mainland. We had spent a great deal of time organising the cockpit controls and indicators for the reverser system, which obviously had to be capable of reaching high reverse thrust levels as quickly as possible after touchdown. The initial proposal from design was to have a throttle box in which the throttles moved through three regions. From an engines idling position, they could be moved forward to max dry power, then further forward through a detent into a reheat arc. To achieve reverse thrust, the throttles had to be pulled back to idle and then lifted over a gate into a third arc, which gave increasing thrust into the reverser buckets with further aft throttle movement.

This arrangement had two major drawbacks. First, by requiring three separate functions within the thrust lever operating arc, the thrust gearing per inch of movement was going to be steep. We feared it might be so steep as to make formation-keeping tricky. And secondly, when trying to achieve high power in reverse rapidly after landing, the pilot was going to be demanding initially an engine spool down as he brought the throttles back through the idle position to reach reverse. Tim Ferguson and I looked at several possibilities and eventually I proposed a system that removed the reverse arc and achieved reverser bucket deployment by rocking the throttles outboard over a detent at any position of the throttle in the dry thrust range. This meant, of course, that the subsequent increase of reverse power was achieved by moving the throttles forward and not rearward in the intuitive sense established on civil aircraft. However, the throttle gearing was kept low by eliminating a separate arc for reverse and reverse thrust could be selected instantly at whatever power setting the pilot had on landing. It was a neat solution and worked well.

The only other fighter-sized aircraft that had used reverse thrust was the Saab Viggen and we had meetings with Saab during our early studies to discuss their experience. Milton Moburg, Saab project pilot for the Viggen, had come to Warton to discuss their reverser experience. They had, in fact, damaged an aircraft badly during reverser development when the pilot lost control directionally on landing. This had been caused by the forward gas plume from the reverser attaching to only one side of the fin when landing in a crosswind. Saab recommended that we fit strakes in the reverser buckets to direct the forward gas flow from the operating buckets outwards away from the fin to avoid any such attachment.

Development of the Tornado reverser system was MBB's responsibility and it worked with Turbo Union (the three-nation engine consortium that produced the RB199 engine) to fit such strakes in both top and bottom reverser buckets. The top strakes were to prevent forward flow attachment to the fin as described above, and the bottom bucket strakes were to move the lower forward gas flow outwards to minimise gas recirculation back into the intakes. MTU produced a working model of the jet pipe and reverser bucket arrangements that, in the wind tunnel, demonstrated the effects of the strakes and from which it was possible to measure the various force vectors. It was during work with this model that a low lip was introduced at the forward edge of the upper buckets to achieve a neutral pitching moment during reverser operation.

In order to permit the shortest possible landing distance it was planned that reverse could be pre-selected by rocking the throttles outboard during the approach to landing. Weight-on-Wheels (WOW) switches prevented the buckets moving until touchdown and, for added safety, indicators were positioned head up in the cockpit that showed the state of the WOW switches. So the reverse landing sequence was: on approach, check WOW indicators show safe. Pre-arm reverse by rocking throttles outboard.

1. The author with SNJ aircraft at Whiting Field, Pensacola, Florida in September 1954.

2. Instructor Lt Cdr Moore USN 'batting' trainees aboard USS *Monterey*.

3. The author's first deck landing, on USS *Monterey* on 25 February 1955. Note the batsman's windbreak behind the aircraft.

4. The North American T28C. 1,425hp Wright Cyclone R1820 engine.

5. The T-28 flight line at Kingsville, Texas, in May 1955.

6. F6F Hellcat bailout trainer at US Naval Air Station Kingsville, Texas, in May 1955. Students had to 'bail out' into a net with the engine at max RPM.

7. A land away with T-28B aircraft at Dallas Naval Air Station in July 1955.

8. Lockheed TV-2. US Navy jet conversion trainer. Allison J33-A-20 turbojet, 4,600lb thrust – a direct descendant of the original Whittle engine.

9. The author with a Grumman F9F-2 Panther at USNAS Kingsville in August 1955. The type had seen service in the Korean War and was then used as an advanced fighter trainer. It had a Pratt & Whitney J48 engine of 5,950lb thrust that was based on the Rolls-Royce Nene.

10. A de Havilland Vampire T.22 jet trainer at RNAS Ford in November 1955. The type had a DH Goblin 35 engine of 3,500lb thrust.

11. Hawker Sea Hawks at RNAS Lossiemouth in April 1956. The type was a successful RN fighter-bomber throughout the 1960s and was powered by a Rolls-Royce Nene 103 engine of 5,300lb thrust.

12. The deck-landing mirror on HMS *Victorious* in 1959.

13. A Fairey Firefly AS Mk.5 at RANAS Nowra in 1956. The aircraft was used by the RAN for observer training and was powered by a Rolls-Royce Griffon engine of 1,730hp.

14. A Hawker Sea Fury FB.11 at RANAS Nowra in 1957. Powered by a Bristol Centaurus engine of 2,450hp, this fighter-bomber development of the Tempest was one of the fastest piston fighters ever built and saw service in Korea.

15. *Left:* CAA Gover RAN at RANAS Nowra in September 1957 displaying a For Valour medal for flying in a Firefly after he had changed the engine.

16. *Bottom:* Australian Naval aerobatic team, Sea Furies, en route from Nowra to Broken Hill in October 1957.

17. A view of formation aerobatics from a Sea Venom over RNAS Yeovilton in June 1961.

18. A Sea Vixen Mk2 refuels from an Argosy C Mk1 at Boscombe Down in January 1966.

19. A Buccaneer Mk1 awaits a hands-off, steam catapult launch during carrier suitability trials in 1961.

20. A Lightning F.53 for the Royal Saudi Air Force retracts its undercarriage during tests at Warton in April 1969.

21. *Right:* The author in MRCA prototype P02 at Warton in February 1975.

22. *Bottom*: MRCA prototype P02 takes on fuel from an RAF Victor tanker's centre station in February 1977.

23. MRCA P02 flying at Mach 1.6/620kt over the Irish Sea on 13 June 1975. It was photographed by chase pilot Alan Love from a single-seat chase Lightning.

24. Paul Millett, John Cockburn, Tom Stafford and the author after astronaut Stafford's Tornado flight from Warton in December 1978.

25. Tornado ADV during its first flight on 27 October 1979. The aircraft was taken to Mach 1.25 and proved remarkably trouble-free for a first flight.

26. The first flight of JP233 sub-munition dispensers and camera pods on ZA354 on 23 February 1982. It was an ugly, bulky load that Tornado's flying control system made 'invisible'.

27. MRCA Prototype P03 demonstrating at Farnborough in 1978 with a full load of eight bombs, two 1,500-litre tanks and two ECM pods.

28. Preparing for the first flight of the EAP at Warton on 8 August 1986. The unofficial 'Fly Navy' logo survived for four flights!

29. *Top*: The EAP on Flight 1 on 8 August 1986. It went supersonic and there were absolutely no snags!

30. *Right*: Pete Orme (second from right) becomes the third pilot to fly the EAP in only five days. He is congratulated by John Vincent, executive director EAP; Chris Yeo, chief test pilot; and the author.

31. The author explaining the EAP cockpit to HRH Prince Philip at Farnborough in September 1986. He was keen to try it!

32. The author with Spitfire PR Mk XIX PS915 at Warton in February 1987. The aircraft had been restored by British Aerospace for the Battle of Britain Memorial Flight and three Warton test pilots 'stole a ride' before it was handed over.

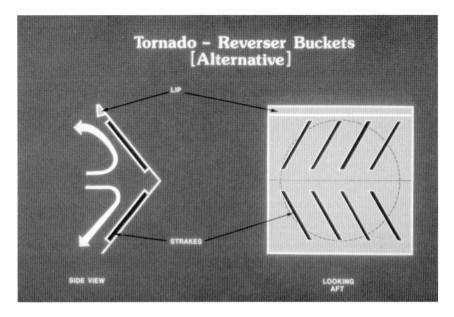

The reverser bucket showing upper and lower strakes and top lip.

Continue to use throttles on the approach as normal. On touchdown, the buckets close automatically and the spoilers on both wings extend as lift dumpers. Slam to max dry power.

MBB carried out tests at Manching to determine at what speed during the landing roll out the forward gas flow from maximum reverse power began to be recirculated into the intakes. Chalk chips were laid on the runway and cameras recorded this light material being thrown forward and sucked into the intakes. The minimum speed reached without any sort of recirculation was 60 knots and at that speed an audio warning signal was brought in to warn the pilot to throttle to idle.

On MRCA's first flight, Paul Millet had used reverse at idle only and not pre-armed, but we quickly made it the normal landing routine and it proved to be very effective. However, we had two problems with it. The first involved insufficient locking pin interference in the arrangements for locking the buckets in for normal flight. We had several nuisance warnings of buckets unlocked in the air and then one day, test pilot Russ Pengelly had one reverser bucket actually deploy in the air in aircraft P06 at 525 knots at 5,300ft. The locking pin was still in effect in the locked position in a badly set up system. He throttled that engine to idle and we advised him not to shut it down in case there might be some residual pneumatic pressure at that setting that was attempting to retract the bucket. The worrying aspect was that, even with high power on the good engine, the airspeed was slowly reducing as he returned to Warton. However, it stabilised eventually and he made an uneventful, single-engine landing. Modifications to the locking gear were speeded up and the problem did not reoccur.

The other problem was more serious and led to an unnecessary (in my opinion) reduction in aircraft performance in service. We began to use pre-armed reverse from quite early in the programme and at high reverse power setting we all experienced directional instability. I particularly remember our first appearance at the Farnborough Air Show in September 1976 when we pre-armed to achieve the best short landing possible. We had developed the technique of pre-arming and then slamming to max dry power just before touchdown. This meant that the reverser buckets closed on accelerating engines and max reverse was achieved within a second or so. There was no significant crosswind and the landings were spectacularly short, but the aircraft would yaw first one way and then the other and required some fancy footwork on the brakes to keep it nominally straight on the runway. We were in deep discussion with design and engineering on this and there were thoughts of feeding the yaw rate signal into the nosewheel steering system to help. Then, later that year, Tim Ferguson, landing P03 on a wet Warton runway, experienced the same problem, lost directional control, ran off the

Landing gear damage to P03 at Warton.

runway, hit a low concrete plinth and collapsed the landing gear. The problem was looked at more seriously.

The directional instability was determined to be caused by random reverse flow attachment/detachment to the fin, in spite of the strakes fitted in the buckets to prevent just that. It was decided to remove the upper strakes and deliberately attach the forward flow firmly to both sides of the fin. And in addition the plan to use a yaw rate feed to the nosewheel steering system was accepted.

With the reverser system responsibility being MBB's, the testing of the revised arrangements was carried out initially at Manching and the results were reported to be good. A full power reverse landing was straight as a die. But when we flew the first modified example at Warton we found that when reverse was pre-armed, which brought the reverser in to play with the nosewheel still off the ground, there was now a significant nose down pitching moment that made for a hard derotation. Warton flight test found this was regularly producing very high nose leg loads and so reverse selection was restricted to after derotation. Engineering indicated that the removal of the strakes from the reverser buckets had altered the system pitching moment, and that aspect had not been reviewed during the change. Pitching moment during reverse operation had initially been set by choice of profile of the bucket lips.

While I argued with engineering that we should be reinstating the reverser model to find a new profile that would return us to a neutral pitching moment, we introduced a landing limitation requiring no reverse selection with the nosewheel off the ground. Introducing a limitation to 'temporarily' get round an engineering or design problem is often the only way forward in a development programme. But as feared, this limitation went with the aircraft into service in a slightly softened but more complicated form, and no further work was done to restore what had been Tornado's remarkable, simple and highly effective landing performance.

Tornado's appearance at Farnborough that year (1976) proved to be a very successful step in the aircraft's first appearance on the display circuit. Paul and I shared the week's flying in P06 and the aircraft stayed serviceable throughout. The routine we flew involved a high rate rotation after lift-off and on the first public demonstration this caused a noisy engine surge with a burst of flame and a brief over-temperature. Rolls-Royce, whose guest chalet was on the front row at Farnborough and close to the runway, was shown at close hand that its RB199 development still had a little way to go. But as usual, it demonstrated its superb support by installing a new engine overnight and in time for engine run checks first thing the following morning.

In early 1977 P02 was involved in high-speed flutter work and we were helped enormously by an RAF Victor tanker being made available in the vicinity of our supersonic corridor down the Irish Sea. Flutter checks consist of causing a structural disturbance in the wing (or tail) by firing a pyrotechnic charge (nicknamed 'bonkers'), and checking that the resulting cyclical distortion is damped at all aircraft speeds. Our routine was to reach around 35,000ft in the area of south-west Scotland and accelerate to supersonic speed on a southerly heading, under the control of Warton Radar. The track south took us between the Irish coast and the Isle of Man, with enough separation from both coasts to ensure no supersonic shock wave could reach them. We would set up a target speed, say Mach 1.8, run the data recorders, fire our 'bonker' structural-excitation gear, hold the test conditions for thirty seconds and then decelerate and turn to top-up fuel with the Victor Tanker (see colour plate 22). The data from the run was telemetered back to base as well as recorded on board, and during our rendezvous with the tanker, it was checked on the ground by our engineers to confirm that the damping was as predicted. If this was confirmed we would be cleared to repeat the run at a higher speed. This use of telemetry, flight refueling and almost real-time analysis allowed us to progress through several test points on each flight and the three or four hour sortie lengths were only limited by the number of shots available in our 'bonker exciters'.

There was always some nail biting at the higher Mach numbers when the test point was finished because the aircraft had to be kept heading down the cleared supersonic route until it became subsonic, allowing us to turn back towards land. I chickened out and diverted to RAF Valley with fuel gauges close to the stops on one occasion, and Paul, with a similar situation, turned early for the tanker and planted a bang on North Wales. Some unexplained damage to a remote chapel was reported.

The initial part of the Tornado development programme was funded on a 'cost-plus' basis until an agreed stage of development had been reached. Thereafter, the contract changed to fixed price. Payment for the programme was made by NAMMA, the NATO MRCA Management Agency, to Panavia, the tri-national company co-ordinating the three partner companies. Payment was triggered initially by demonstration of specific programme milestones and three of the early ones were the achievement of the design Vne (never exceed speed) in three wing sweeps: 500 knots IAS with wing fully forward at 25 degrees, Mach 1.4/640 knots at 45-degree wing and

800 knots IAS at 67 degrees, full sweep. The 25-degree wing point was demonstrated early in the programme without difficulty. As the early engines were down on thrust, the 45-degree wing point of Mach 1.4/640 knots had to be accelerated with the wing fully swept, and the wing then swept forward to 45 degrees when on condition. The aircraft would not, at that early engine standard, maintain that speed but slowly decelerated. The flight was chased by a Lightning flown by Alan Love, a popular member of the flight ops team who had flown Lightnings with the RAF and who was tragically killed later in the programme in a Buccaneer accident at West Freugh range. Alan was chasing the point to observe the event and afterwards presented me with a photograph of P02 at the target speed. He confided that he had problems with his small camera while taking it and was forced to use both hands while flying the Lightning with his knees! (See colour plate 23.)

The 800-knot milestone was also memorable. This time it was flown by Paul Millett and I monitored it from the flight test console. As usual, we had hot-mike contact between pilot and console and we had full instrument readout on the console as Paul dived on to the point. He read out the airspeed as he approached the point, '790, 795, 800, 800, 800 …' but my instrumentation on the console was indicating, '790, 795, 800, 805, 810 …' I called him to chop the power but he maintained his confident readouts of '800, 800' for another five seconds or so as the airspeed continued to increase in his gentle descent. And it was with some reluctance that he throttled back as requested. The incident was looked at and eventually explained. P02, our first prototype, and also P03, were fitted with head-down conventional instruments, since the planned head-up display was not yet available. The specification we had given to the instrument maker for our non-standard layout was that the air-speed indicator should read 'from 75 to 800 knots'. And so it did.

After what seemed like a slow start to the MRCA flying programme in 1974, with just P01 in West Germany and P02 in Britain, 1975 saw four more prototypes in the air: P03 at Warton in August, P04 in Manching, West Germany in September, P05 in Caselle, Italy, in early December and P06 at Warton just before Christmas. P07 followed in West Germany in March 1976, the last British prototype, P08, in July that year, and the second Italian prototype, P09, in February 1977. The early flying rates were inevitably low. Development of the new RB199 engine held back progress of the flight programme and delays due to engine problems were common in the first two years. Problems occurred with turbine blade cooling and separately with internal oil seals. The sensitivity of the engine instrumentation surprised us all and was helpful in engine health checking. On one occasion a post-flight inspection showed a single, burnt-out turbine blade (some blades were so small that the loss of a complete blade did not cause an imbalance detectable in the cockpit). By playing back the instrumentation trace of turbine blade temperature it was possible to detect a very small jump in the trace at the moment the blade burnt off.

The nine prototypes had been allocated separate tasks, though with inevitably a little overlap. It had been intended that the test pilots in the programme should get involved with the programmes at each test base, though once each country had all its prototypes flying, this aim petered out. I flew a German prototype at Manching only twice, and an Italian one never. My experience in Germany made me feel that our flight-testing environment and organisation at Warton were in good shape comparatively.

It was in Germany that I first became aware that the different aerospace companies had widely differing relationships between their flight operations departments and engineering. At Warton, Bee as chief test pilot in the early days of Canberra and Lightning development had proved to be such a valuable (and dominating) member of the development team that he carved a significant place for his flight operations department within the Warton organisation. He was made a director of British Aircraft Corporation (Preston) in 1965 and this position of director flight operations at BAE Systems continues to this day, giving the test pilot a significant voice within the company. In Germany I found that the flight operations department, headed by the chief test pilot (in my Tornado days, Fred Rammensee followed by Peter Weger), was under the control of the engineering director and as a consequence was often prevented from giving untrammelled opinions about an aircraft's performance or handling. In Italy, although the test pilots were regarded rather as Gods, they too had formal opinions filtered by an engineering or project director.

During the development of an aircraft there will inevitably be situations where the test pilot's opinion leads to requests for change, and this is challenged by engineering or the manager of the programme, who has the overall cost to consider. I recall that one of our tutors at ETPS, Sqn Ldr Eddie Rigg, gave a lecture titled 'Conferencemanship', outlining the likely tactics that those of us who would go into industry as test pilots might meet when an agreement was being sought on changes that test pilots had requested. The number one tactic for the engineers was, 'Don't invite the test pilots to the meeting!'

During the Tornado programme there was much (healthy) discussion on the way forward during the early MRCA flight-testing at Warton but during it all I always found the technical and project directors, Ollie Heath and Gerrie Willox, very anxious to discuss the detail of the problem and to understand the pilot point of view before reaching a conclusion.

As the programme built up there was inevitably a continuous stream of senior defence officials from the three participating air forces and the West German Navy, all anxious to fly in the aircraft. The Panavia company insisted that all such requests must be authorised by it in order to thin out the queue and so minimise interference with the programme. In October 1977, Dr John Gilbert, then the UK Minister of State for Defence, became the first government minister to fly in the aircraft. He came up to Warton and I flew him in the rear seat of P03 on a fifty-minute sortie of general handling, including some supersonics and low-level flight over the low-level range in North Wales. This was obviously simply parliamentary box ticking but, with occasional sniping at the programme by the press on economic grounds, it was useful political support.

Also during 1977 we had a social visit to the company from Buzz Aldrin, who with Neil Armstrong had taken the Apollo 11 trip to the moon in July 1969 and was the second man to walk on it. Ollie Heath (our engineering director), Paul Millet and I dined Buzz and his then girlfriend at a hotel in Southport. He enjoyed talking about his fighter pilot days during the Korean War as much as he did reminiscing about his moon shot.

Dr Gilbert, UK Minister of Defence, the author and Lord Beswick, chairman of BAe, after the minister's flight in P03 in October 1977.

In January 1978 we squeezed into the busy flight test programme an evaluation of the aircraft by a team of Canadian test pilots. Canada at that time was looking for a replacement of its F–104s, CF–101s and CF–5s for NATO and home defence duties and the Tornado was on its shortlist of six. The team visited MBB and Aeritalia before coming to Warton to observe and join in our test-flying programme. We ran an intensive briefing course for the Canadian team that consisted of two pilots, two navigators, an engineer and a team leader. Rolls-Royce Bristol sent up a senior engineer to give them a detailed briefing on the engine and I remember wincing when, after describing the overall layout of the RB199 engine, he said, 'Actually, if we were starting the design over again, we wouldn't go for a three-spool layout.' The Canadians flew in the front and back seats and sampled the full flight envelope we had cleared to that point. At that time we were just discovering a surge tendency in the right engine above Mach 1.8 that was subsequently found to be caused by an intake swirl, eventually fixed with a strake at the intake elbow. The Canadians were impressed with the performance we had covered to that date but we were unable to show them Mach 2. In May that year, I joined a sales team from Panavia giving briefings in Winnipeg and Montreal on the programme's results so far and the aircraft's performance. We were offering work share if the Canadians chose Tornado for its new fighter but they eventually chose the F–18, which was already in production and so would be available earlier.

In March 1978 the programme received the first –4 standard engine and it was first flown in P01 at Manching. At Warton we began to change our –3 standards for the –4s in the early summer and the ongoing programme of flutter checks, using P02, P03 and later, P15, speeded up as the supersonic test points were now easier to reach with the increased thrust. We had managed to reach Mach 1.9 with the –3s but it was a struggle to get there before the fuel was down to dangerously low levels.

In parallel with the Tornado programme, the two Buccaneers continued with the avionic system development but, on 5 July 1978, we lost test pilot Alan Love, navigator Roy Bigland and Buccaneer XN285 in an accident at the West Freugh range, just south of Stranraer. Alan had arrived at the range early for his 'slot' and had been simply waiting in a low-level, low-speed holding pattern, conserving fuel, when the aircraft stalled. This was our first serious accident at Warton and naturally it was a huge blow. Alan had first joined the company specifically to do production testing on Lightning aircraft and had been involved in many deliveries of that aircraft to Saudi Arabia. Following that programme he had shared the flying of the company's executive aircraft and then completed a Buccaneer conversion course to join John Cockburn on the Buccaneer avionic development programme. Roy Bigland had been an observer in the navy before joining ESAMS, the avionics integration group run by Elliotts. He had been involved in the design as well as the testing of the navigation and weapon system from early in the programme.

During the mid-1970s, the US Air Force was itself looking to develop a low-level strike aircraft and announced its Enhanced Tactical Fighter (ETF) programme. The announced specification was very much like that of the Tornado from a performance and weapon delivery capability point of view. The main shortfall was in sortie range and the Panavia organisation began to investigate ways of improving this and prepared bid proposals. In December 1978, Gen. Tom Stafford, USAF Deputy Chief of Staff, Research, Development and Acquisition, came over to Warton to fly the aircraft – the first American to do so (see colour plate 24).

Stafford, as Astronaut Commander of Apollo 10, had been in command of the first lunar orbit and reconnaissance prior to the first moon landing by Apollo 11. So there were some wry smiles when George McAuley, our chief navigator and an expert in the Tornado back seat navigation systems, began his briefing to Tom (who was about to fly in the back seat of P08) with the words, 'Well Sir. I'm going to assume you know nothing about navigation.' Tom was flown through our dummy low-level attack circuit by John Cockburn and gave a very complimentary debrief on the aircraft handling and systems. Several of us were later involved in giving briefings in the Pentagon and at SAC Headquarters to further the Tornado case for the ETF buy, but the Americans simply modified their F-15 to a similar capability to produce the Strike Eagle to fill the programme. I later had one flight in the F-15 fighter version and felt that the low-level ride of this undoubtedly fine fighter was not a patch on the smooth ride in Tornado with the wings swept (sweeping the wing not only softens off the lift curve slope but also tucks away about 5 per cent of the wing area into the fuselage, increasing the wing loading).

During 1978 and for the first half of 1979, Tornado activity at Warton increased as P06 started its gun-firing development and was used to investigate directional stability, while P02 continued supersonic flutter checks up to the 800 knots IAS limit. Then, on 12 June, we suffered the first loss of a Tornado prototype and its crew when Russ Pengelly and Sqn Ldr John Gray were lost in the Irish Sea during a weapon system development flight.

Russ had been with us at Warton for only two years and was already recognised as a most talented test pilot. Paul Millett and I had first seen his remarkable aerobatic capabilities at the Farnborough Air Show some four years earlier when he had demonstrated the Lightning there for the RAF. In particular, his very accurate low-level Derry turns were highly impressive. He had then taken the Empire Test Pilots' Course at Boscombe Down and had completed a tour of testing there. When the pace of testing increased at Warton, requiring an extra pilot, we thought first of Russ and were delighted that he was keen to join us. I flew him in our two-stick Tornado, P03, in September 1977 and he was clearly up to speed quickly. We asked him to work up in Tornado display flying and he began to give some outstanding demonstrations of the aircraft in front of our continuous stream of VIP visitors.

Sqn Ldr Gray was the lead RAF navigator for the Tornado flight test programme at Boscombe Down and had flown with us at Warton many times. He was an expert on the aircraft's navigation and weapon system and had been on one of his frequent working visits.

On that day, 12 June, I was doing lateral handling with P03 and had planned to come back to the Warton circuit on completion to practise a demonstration to be given at RAF Waddington at the end of that week (Russ was also working up a display he was to give at the International Air Tattoo at Greenham Common). But when I got back down to low level and had a look at the weather in the circuit area I found it was not suitable for display practice, with mist reducing visibility to between 1 and 2 miles. I landed and shortly afterwards heard that Russ Pengelly and John Gray in P08 were missing. Air traffic control had been monitoring their activities in Liverpool Bay and reported that they had disappeared from radar and could not be raised on radio.

Russ had been tasked with checking out one aspect of the weapons system. He had set up a circuit at low level over the Irish Sea, running south towards Liverpool Bay, with radar locked on to a buoy as target, and pulling up to simulate release of a bomb in a toss manoeuvre. He had completed one such circuit and in setting up a second he descended visually in a left hand turn on to the southerly run-in heading, but flew into the sea in those misty conditions. It was an enormous blow to the programme and, of course, to the families concerned.

The MoD accident organisation brought in a dredger to pull out the wreckage from the Irish Sea and eventually it found the recorders including the cockpit voice recorder. This told us that Russ and John were busy setting up the run-in conditions when they hit, and convinced me that Russ was judging his altitude visually. In making this visual judgment of height, pilots instinctively absorb the position of the horizon. When the horizon is low down you feel you are high and could fly lower. But reduced visibility conditions also lower the horizon and my personal feeling was that this phenomenon had caught Russ out.

During the second half of 1979, our first Tornado Air Defence Variant (ADV) was completing construction. The ADV had been ordered only by the UK as a long-range interceptor for the RAF. Its main offensive armament was the Skyflash missile and it carried four of them, semi-submerged under the belly. The main fuselage had been lengthened to create space for this, and to accommodate increased fuel and additional weapon system avionics. The radome now had to cater for not two radar dishes but the one air intercept radar, and the resulting slimmer nose was expected to reduce drag. Roy Kenward and I made the first flight on 27 October and confirmed that it was more slippery than the original strike version. We had hoped that there would be nothing stopping us taking it supersonic on its first flight and indeed there wasn't. We had taken a long schedule of points to cover, and since everything worked well we flew for over an hour and a half and worked our way up to Mach 1.2. Of course, the aircraft was around 85 per cent unchanged from the strike version we knew well, but the pitch control was changed to reduce stick forces slightly and so were the fuel system and the flap system. The stick forces in the basic Tornado were a little heavier than we liked in the UK but the other two partners were used to American stick forces in their F-104s and F-4s so we had lost the battle to keep it light. But when the ADV design was opened up to insert a plug in the fuselage to increase the length, the pitch feel unit had to be moved and since ADV was UK only, we asked for a slight reduction in stick force per G (in fact, the later introduction of the spin prevention system effectively increased pitch stick manoeuvring forces again). (See colour plate 25.)

The most noticeable change was the improvement in acceleration rate when supersonic and within ten months of this first flight we were exploring handling at Mach 2, helped by the new Mk 104 engines.

In 1979, in an effort to increase interest in Tornado from the USAF, Panavia sent a party to the USA to give presentations on its capability to the Pentagon and SAC Headquarters. From Warton, John Weston and I gave briefings on the design and the operations respectively and I was asked to write an article for *Air Force Magazine*, describing the way the aircraft systems worked on a typical bombing sortie (see Appendix 3: Flying an 800-Knot Tornado).

Early in 1980 we started on that most interesting programme to the test pilot: spinning. Tornado was to have a spin prevention system to give it some degree of carefree handling. In other words, the aircraft's own systems should prevent the pilot stalling it in harsh manoeuvring. A Spin Prevention and Incidence Limiting System (SPILS) was designed to achieve this. It was necessary to carry out some spin departures to fully understand the aircraft's stall/spin boundary and susceptibility. P02 and P03 were fitted with an anti-spin chute gantry for recovery help in the event that, as expected, the trials proved that spin recovery was difficult. P02 was the primary airplane with P03 as back up and, in fact, P03 was never spun.

During the autumn of 1979 the three pilots to be involved, Paul Millett, Jerry Lee and myself, joined the engineers in a visit to the French vertical wind tunnel in Lille to witness some of the spin model testing. The vertical wind tunnel was a large diameter (about 15ft) cylinder on a vertical axis, with a large fan mounted at its upper end, driven by a Merlin engine. Aircraft models were skilfully flicked into the rising airflow, in a spinning condition, from a gallery one level up from the large air intake at ground level. The 'driver' of the fan also sat in this gallery and was able to vary the air flow in such a way as to keep the spinning model in sight at gallery level. A coarse net hung below the gallery and collected the aircraft model if the aircraft descent rate increased suddenly, as when the spin stopped.

The models were made with appropriate centres of gravity and aerodynamic accuracy and could be signalled by radio to make a configuration change while spinning. So tailplane angle could be varied, as could wing spoiler angles and rudder. Wing sweep could be altered between drops. The ultimate fairground toy! Information from these experiments confirmed the various modes of spin, including a 'fast flat spin' with the wing swept, which we thankfully never saw in real life. Information from these tunnel tests was used to brief the pilots on spin recovery techniques and confirmed that recovery procedure in all wing sweeps (from the fully developed spin) was to be opposite rudder and full *back* stick; in other words, the opposite stick position to the classic normal recovery one. (Recovery action immediately on entry to a spin was, as always, to centralise everything.) Full back stick moves the tailplane leading edge down, unblanking the fin and so allowing it to do its job of countering the yaw.

In December 1979 we all had a refresher spin trip in the ETPS Hunter at Boscombe Down and in February 1980 the Tornado spinning programme began. The area chosen for the spin trial was over land, so that if we were not able to recover and had to eject, the aircraft, or what was left of it, would be recoverable for investigation. So an uninhabited area in the North Yorkshire moors was chosen, close to our base, so giving good telemetry signal strength back to Warton. We had quite stringent weather conditions to meet – good visibility, of course, and no spinning above complete cloud cover so the direction of aircraft rotation could be recognised clearly. The routine was to climb the aircraft to 42,000ft and pull up to swap the excess airspeed for more height while turning on to the planned start heading and setting up the planned configuration. We always flew with a Hunter chase aircraft and a cine photographer, and the Hunter would try to follow us down in the spin, filming if he could, and manoeuvring as required to keep the Tornado in close view, but out of his way! The chase task was at least as tricky as the spin test.

Tornado P02 had been fitted with an emergency power unit (EPU), a mono fuel unit as fitted to the standard F-16, which was to start automatically and power the aircraft electrics and hydraulics in the event of the expected engines flame out. In addition, there were cockpit cameras positioned on the right side of the ejection seat, which could capture some of the instrument panel activity and some of the outside world through the windscreen.

The weather limitations slowed down the programme somewhat but we eventually achieved about twenty spinning sorties in the three main wing sweep angles and with and without airbrake. Spin entry was achieved by holding full back stick and dictating the nose slice direction with rudder. Both engines invariably overheated on entry and had to be shut down and the EPU proved reliably able to take over the hydraulic and electrical load. The spin motion was mainly in yaw with a little superimposed pitching and rolling. Yaw rate was moderately high but steady with the wing forward and more oscillatory when swept. The stick was put back to central during the spin and full back stick was put in for recovery. This input led to eventual spin recovery in all wing sweep cases but, of course, the tricky part was then to recognise when to get the stick back to central to avoid starting the spin again.

Each pilot resorted to use of the anti-spin chute at least once during his share of the fun and, of course, once that was pulled and the chute discarded, we had to forego further tests on that sortie and go home.

Data from the spinning trials was used to plan the angle of attack and yaw values at which the SPILS system was to begin to limit the pilot's authority in those two channels during hard manoeuvring. The system could be switched off and there was much discussion when the aircraft went into service as to whether it was a plus or a nuisance. I remember that when SPILS was first fitted I became somewhat anxious during an aerobatic display at low level at Farnborough, when holding full back stick and pointing at the ground at around 1,200ft. But it undoubtedly lets the pilot get straight to maximum performance safely if bounced into hard manoeuvring.

In July 1980, Paul Millet and I delivered the first two Tornados to the Tri-National Tornado Training Establishment (TTTE) at RAF Cottesmore. Here the pilots and navigators of the three NATO customers, West Germany, Italy and the UK, were to be trained over the coming years. Paul flew in with Ollie Heath, our engineering systems director, in the rear seat, and he was to do the formal handover of the aircraft. I had previously done a fly-by with the aircraft at Cottesmore in May when the airfield was officially opened for this task, and now the first aircrews were settling in and starting their groundschool. The base was tri-nationally funded and tri-nationally run, and it was to be equipped with Tornados from Italy and Germany as well as from the UK. The school was well run and frequently made the point that the total integration of the three air forces there meant that any of the students, be he German, Italian or British, could be flying an aircraft owned by any of the three air forces and with an instructor from any of those air forces in the back seat.

In 1980 there was also an increase in the number of top-ranking officers coming to industry to fly in the aircraft to assess it. In September I flew Gen. Kelly Burke over our terrain following route up the west coast from Warton to Barrow-in-Furness, then north-east, terrain-following through the Lake District, and back south through the Yorkshire Dales before climbing for some high-level handling. Gen. Burke was the USAF Deputy Chief of Staff, Research, Development and Acquisition. We flew one of the first production standard trainers and as he said in his debrief, 'We did it all!' From the rear seat he sampled terrain following, wing sweeping, target acquisition using the radar, aerobatics and supersonics. Finally, he did some landings at Warton and excited our PR men after landing by suggesting that the Tornado was about fifteen years more advanced than their own low-level strike aircraft, the F-111.

In October we flew Gen. Mathis, the USAF Vice Chief of the Air Staff, and in November, Jerry Lee flew Gen. Brickel, Deputy Chief of Staff Research and Development, USAF. All claimed to be very impressed with what we had produced. In the same time period, Manlio Quarantelli, the Aeritalia chief

The author with Gen.
Mathis, USAF Strategic
Air Command, during
a Tornado demo in
October 1980.

test pilot, was flying Gen. Mura of the Italian Air Force and Dietrich Seeck from MBB was flying the German Navy's Admiral Bethge. In all these cases we flew the VIP in the rear seat of a two-sticker and although some of them were in good flying practice, it would have taken several days' briefing to bring them up to a safe enough level of understanding of the aircraft to let them fly it from the front seat.

While discussing flying VIPs, I must make mention of flying with Bee, or Roland Beamont, BAC's director of flight operations when I joined the company. By the time I arrived at Warton, Bee had already retired from flying, but he took a very active interest in all flight operations. I remember he met me as I climbed out of the cockpit after my first Lightning trip, anxious to hear the new boy's impression of the fighter he had had so much influence on.

In July 1969, after my first year at Warton and with experience now in Lightning, Canberra and Jet Provost, I was to fly a sortie in the Saudi

Strikemaster doing some checks on the new gunsight installation. The Strikemaster was a beefed-up development of the standard RAF jet trainer, the Jet Provost, a side-by-side two-seater. Warton was hosting a visit from a local pensioners' group that day and I was asked to carry out a brief flying display after take-off for them. Bee, who had been involved in briefing the group earlier, came into the operations office and said he would like to come with me on the trip. At the briefing he asked if he could take over the flying of the demo; who was I to do anything but agree! Bee took over after take-off and I then sat back and watched as he threw the aircraft around using every inch of available stick movement in all axes. I had done a deal of solo demonstration flying in the navy, in Sea Vixen and Buccaneer aircraft, but never by dealing so apparently belligerently with the stick! Every roll into or out of a turn was made with full stick and every pitch change was snapped into. After landing we discussed his demo technique and the difference in his view between demonstrating an aircraft to an observer in the aircraft – all smoothness – and to those outside on the ground – highest rate attitude changes. I learned a good deal from the old master who had wakened up the Farnborough Air Show with his fabled demonstrations of the Canberra and Lightning prototypes in earlier years. I was given the Strikemaster to demonstrate at Farnborough the following year and got his nodded approval.

As mentioned previously, Bee had a very distinguished wartime career flying Typhoons and Tempests before taking up test flying during that fascinating time of investigation of the effects of Mach number on the high-speed fighters of the day, i.e. the Meteor and the Vampire. The English Electric Company at Warton, the forerunner of BAC and BAe, had been awarded a contract to investigate transonic effects on the Meteor during the winter of 1947 and Bee had been given the job. The company was already well advanced in its design work on the Canberra and the results of the compressibility investigation that Bee undertook were to be used in its concept of a next generation fighter that would be capable of intercepting it! As English Electric's chief test pilot, he went on to manage and lead the flight development of the highly successful Canberra and the remarkable supersonic Lightning, which certainly proved up to the task of taking it on. In my day we were all asked into his office at odd times to explain comments in our flight reports and he was a master of the technique of continuing to ask more and more detailed questions until he finally plumbed the depth of your knowledge of the subject in hand and you had to resort to the old naval stopper of, 'I don't know sir, but I'll find out.'

Bee, too, wanted to fly in a Tornado and argued that as director of flight operations for Panavia, he must. And so on 13 August 1975 I had the pleasure of taking him for a handling flight in the back seat of the two-sticker, P03. At this stage of the development of the flying control system we were still experiencing tendencies towards pilot induced oscillation (PIO) in pitch. PIO is a phenomenon of over-control caused by an inappropriate control response to the result of a previous control input. It can be caused, for example, by aircraft system delayed response, as in actuator rate limiting, or by a control system with too high a gain, triggering a human pilot over-response. At the time of Bee's flight, we had already progressed from an early standard of pitch computer that had produced PIO tendencies, to the next standard, which was better but still to be improved. (In Italy, prototype P05 suffered a heavy landing in January 1976, when Peter Trevisan experienced a PIO on landing from a test flight.)

In Bee's fascinating book *Fighter Test Pilot*, published in 1986, he describes our flight in P03 in some detail and claims to have noted, from his back-seat position, a lateral PIO (i.e. in roll) during my landing from that sortie. Now the early lateral computer did indeed produce a PIO tendency and the test pilots from all three companies began to examine this and called for improvement. When there seemed to be reluctance on the part of the Control and Stability Augmentation System (CSAS) team to examine this criticism, we called upon Bee as director flight operations, to raise it at a senior level. This he did (and a further and final improvement to the lateral computer was made), but, not untypically, he describes in his book the 'discovery' of this flaw as having been his own as he watched the landing from the rear seat. I challenged this 'memory' when his book first appeared and we exchanged gentle opposing views on it in correspondence for some months.

Increasingly during 1978 and afterwards, we examined the handling of Tornado with a huge variety of external loads. My logbook shows handling with 4 × Kormoran missiles (November 1978), 4 × BL755s (July 1979), buddy/buddy refuelling pod (September 1979), 12 × 1,000lb bombs (November 1980) and eventually the largest store of all, the JP233 'concrete dibber', which was carried initially in February 1982 and was then subject to jettison and firing trials in June 1982. As already described, the Tornado flying control system very much minimised the effects on handling that the various stores imposed. However, the secondary effects of such manoeuvres as rapid rolling with a heavy wing load and under G could give some interesting effects. By the 1970s, of course, the mathematical modelling techniques available meant that only very rarely were the results of the planned tests unexpected, though I recall on several occasions coming back to discuss unusual outcomes (see colour plate 26).

During early 1980 the first production Tornados began to appear on the flight line, and from the first they were remarkably serviceable. We devised a production flight test schedule that initially required three to four flights to complete, but as time went on we rarely needed more than three flights to clear all performance and system checks. Our chief production test pilot was Eric Bucklow, who had been production testing Canberra, Strikemaster and Jaguar, and flew anything he could get his hands on including our Cessna and HS.125 executive aircraft. In March that year he took on the Tornado production testing too, and flew many of the first flights of the Tornados coming off the production line. On his fiftieth such first flight we had a small ceremony to record that event and since he was a teetotaler we simply replaced the traditional champagne with a bottle of milk!

Also in 1980 the Royal Navy announced the reforming of the Naval Reserve Air Branch. Former Fleet Air Arm aircrew under 50 years of age could apply to join and retrain on fast jets for two weeks a year. I went to talk to our managing director, making the obvious case that it would be very helpful for our company to have such an 'in' to current military flying, and put my uniform back on for the inaugural dinner in the wardroom of RNAS Yeovilton in July.

The author presents Eric Bucklow, chief production test pilot, with a bottle of milk after his fiftieth first production test flight. Behind them are John Squier and Les Hurst, and to the right is Eric's navigator, Al Smith.

My first spell of 'retraining' started at Yeovilton in February 1981, with dual 'refamil' flights in the Hunter T.8 before getting back into the single-seat Hunter GA.11 for low-level navigation practice and 2in rocketing again at the familiar Lilstock Range on the Bristol Channel. Bliss! I shouldn't say that it was good to be back with 'enjoyable' flying again, but it was certainly a welcome change to have a simpler focus and be able to 'look over the side' a bit more – and there was no report writing!

Yeovilton at this time was home base to the Sea Harrier squadrons, and though there would be no opportunity to fly them, we could mix it with them on an almost daily basis, which was good for the Harrier pilots to practise their dissimilar-type combat skills and good for us 'wrinklies' to be able to try to get back up to combat scratch in our ancient Hunters. The Harrier pilots we were 'playing with' soon became household names when they were embarked in HMS *Invincible* to retake the Falkland Islands the following year. I remember particularly some steely one v one combat with Cdr 'Sharkey' Ward on 5 March 1981. We in the reserve fully expected to be 'called up' during the Falklands crisis, not to go out to the 'sharp end' but to perhaps fill in some of the home base slots to release current pilots for active duty. It was only after the operation was over that we were told that since war had not actually been formally declared, the government was not able to call us up. The law was to be changed shortly! I very much looked forward to the annual fortnight's flying at Yeovilton each year after that as a break from the more intensive Warton tasks and as a 'refresher' in current service flying tactics – and socialising!

In June 1981 we took the first ADV, A01, to Le Bourget to perform at the Paris Air Show. Paul Kelly flew rear seat for the first seven days and Roy Kenward for the remaining four and the flight back to Warton. Demo flying was an important aspect of the Warton test pilot's job. Farnborough, Paris and the International Air Tattoo (IAT) at Greenham Common (later at Fairford) were the major events, but we also had to cover smaller displays and ad hoc shows for visitors. All low-level aerobatics had to be authorised by the MoD in London and strict rules were set in terms of minimum height and distance from the crowd line. From 1974 until the end of my Warton flying in 1987, I was a member of the Flying Control Committee for the Farnborough and IAT shows, overseeing the safety aspects, and it was of great interest to meet the demo pilots from all around the world. We tend to think of these guys as blatant extroverts but that's not usually the case. They are well-practised, well-briefed professionals whose primary aim is safety. At Warton I found a similar

The author back in
Naval uniform at
RNAS Yeovilton in
February 1981.

situation existed with most of the big firms demonstrating at Farnborough, the main difficulty of putting on a good demonstration flight was getting hold of an aircraft for demo practice in time to work up an attractive routine. We would discuss a sequence, practise it at a safe height and then arrange for someone to watch critically from the ground, making notes for later debrief when it was eventually brought low level. As far as the actual performance is concerned, I have already described Bee Beamont's aggressive style and that was still being talked about by the Farnborough cognoscenti in 1969 when I first went to Farnborough. 'Maximum roll rates when putting on bank or rolling out. Maximum pitch rates when starting or finishing turns. Leave the smooth manoeuvring to the passenger carriers.' The shortage of practice time with the aircraft could be gauged by the degree of improvement of the demo during the week of presentations at Farnborough or Paris.

The Farnborough Air Show, run by the Society of British Aircraft Companies (SBAC), was originally an annual September event but from 1964 alternated every other year with the Paris Air Show. My first show after joining BAC was in September 1970 and it was the last time that the pilots taking part were invited to a pilots' tent lunch each day by the control tower – a fabulous cold buffet arrangement to which all industry test pilots were invited and where we could meet boyhood aviation heroes. In subsequent years we ate lunch in our company's entertaining chalets on the spectator's side of the runway. There was a mass aircrew briefing at 11 a.m. and the flying programme started at 2 p.m. There was always excellent radio discipline at the big shows. Any listener to the tower traffic would be surprised at the lack of chat. The pilot would call for taxi clearance at a pre-briefed time and taxi to the waiting point off the runway. The tower would clear him to 'line up and take off' at his programmed time and the next call would be four-and-a-half or five minutes later, as dictated by the programme, when the pilot would call 'downwind' and be given clearance to land. There was usually a decision to make as to whether you did a good weather or a bad weather show, the latter being flat with no looping manoeuvres. Usually the answer was obvious but occasionally when the weather was mixed and changing constantly you had to play it by ear, an uneasy situation.

We first took Tornado to Farnborough in September 1976. Paul Millett and I shared the flying in P06, which was our single-seater prototype that had the instrumentation normally housed in the gun bays fitted into the rear cockpit. That year we performed alongside the new USAF F-16 fighter, which put on a highly manoeuvrable show. It was clear that we really should have demonstrated our own manoeuvrability with a full weapons load to show Tornado in its normal environment. (In September 1978 I took P03 to Farnborough and this time we carried out a full show with eight 1,000lb-bomb shapes under fuselage and two 1,500-litre tanks and two ECM pods under the wings.) (See colour plate 27.)

On arrival at Farnborough on the Sunday prior to the show week, each pilot had to do a practice show in front of the flying control committee and get approval. In 1976, Paul Millett, then Warton chief test pilot, flew P06 down from Warton, and Jimmy Dell (Director Flight Operations, Panavia) and I flew down in the company's Cessna 420. Jimmy and I leaned on the fence outside the Farnborough tower to watch Paul's approval flight shortly after we arrived. Paul and I had both practised the same routine at home so I knew it backwards. At one point the wing was swept from right forward to fully swept during a pull up into a loop, to show wing movement during manoeuvre, and then back to fully forward (25 degrees) with manoeuvre flap to complete the pull out. I was highly concerned to see that Paul did not sweep back to 25 degrees during the pull out. Still fully swept, he pulled to a higher and higher angle of attack to recover, yawing off to a southerly heading as he pulled and disappeared from view behind the spectator line, to reappear on finals for landing. Paul would never discuss the event and checking the flight test instrumentation later we found the maximum angle of attack could not be read because it was off the scale! He had handled the situation with great skill but must have needed a laundry change afterwards.

The social life in the company chalet during the Farnborough and Paris shows was always a highlight of the week. After one of the later shows in the ADV, when Roy Kenward and I got back to the company chalet for a drink to cool down with, we were met by our company PR manager, who introduced us to a reporter from a Japanese aviation magazine. The Japanese were always very interested in the shows at Farnborough and Paris. We joined this gentleman at the bar, where he may have been standing for some time, and were entertained by his highly enthusiastic questions and comments. But he was so animated that at one stage, without looking, he scooped up a handful of what I guess he thought were peanuts from a dish on the bar and filled his mouth with second-hand olive stones!

BAe support team and crew with ADV A01 at the Farnborough Air Show on 5 September 1980.

Warton Aircrew in January 1981. L–R: Sam Hardy, exec fleet pilot; Pete Orme, test pilot; Derek Leeming, ops manager; John Squier, test pilot and safety equipment; Peter Gordon-Johnson, test pilot; Chris Bowyer, exec fleet pilot; Jim Stuttard, test navigator; Les Hurst, test navigator; Dave Eagles, test pilot; Sandy Aitken, test pilot; Jerry Lee, test pilot; Keith Hartley, test pilot; Don Thomas, test pilot; Paul Millett, test pilot; George McAuley, test navigator; Paul Kelly, test navigator; Al Smith, test navigator; Eric Bucklow, production test pilot; Roy Kenward, test navigator; Chris Yeo, test pilot; Vic Malings, test navigator; Reg Stock, test pilot.

Demo flying at the big shows was always eagerly anticipated, of course. Prior to my first Farnborough show I remember mentally rehearsing the routine continuously as I tried to get to sleep the night before! But with experience the self-confidence grows and the task becomes reduced to the basics of getting the positioning right – not easy with crosswinds or visibilities reduced by cloud or rain. Most of our Warton pilots and navigators became expert and I should add that the presence of the navigator in the Tornado during the routine was always enormously helpful, calling speeds, G level and time to go while the pilot was looking back over his shoulder at the display line.

During 1981 we had several service test pilots and navigators come to Warton from Boscombe Down to do a preview assessment on the Tornado ADV. They flew a five-flight programme in two fighter configurations on A02 and went away happy. These assessments by the customer were, of course, very important to them, to keep a check on how the aircraft was turning out in relation to the specification, but the company was always anxious to minimise the time that they were given in order to keep our own development on schedule.

From our point of view in flight operations, it was a useful time to discuss the programme informally with the assessing crews and to perhaps give our views on areas that we felt could be improved if the customer was to add similar comments to our own internal ones. Whereas in the early part of the programme the company was always willing to make changes that we stated were needed, in this later phase, with the contract now changed from 'cost plus' to 'fixed price', we usually had to argue pretty strenuously for changes that we felt would make the crew's task easier. There was never any reluctance for change if the proposal was a safety issue, but if engineering thought they could answer a costly proposal with a crew procedure change, that was usually their proposed solution. These differences of opinion sometimes got as far as the local board meeting and our then managing director, Frank Roe, always showed great skill in reducing the debate to a sensible balanced level.

In June, we had an enjoyable diversion when an exercise to refurbish the sole surviving example of the English Electric Company's Wren aircraft finally came to the flight test stage.

The Wren had been the company's entry to a competition in the 1920s for a light economical aircraft with (I think) a 9hp Jap engine and Paul Millet and I were invited to fly it. I had two short sorties on 1 June and it certainly

The author in the English Electric Wren at Warton in June 1981.

defined the bottom end of the power-to-weight ratio spectrum for me! On that no-wind day it took about 800yd to get airborne and some six minutes to reach 500ft. I remember setting it up for a stall there and was impressed to experience an almost instantaneous transfer from virtually level flight to a 90-degree dive. The Wren is now part of the Shuttleworth Collection of old aircraft at Old Warden.

It was also in 1981 that Paul and I had invitations to fly the F-15 and F-16 with the USAF in West Germany. My sortie in the rear seat of the F-15 from the USAF base at Bitburg was disappointingly short due to a fuel leak that developed during the trip. The all-round view from the cockpit and the general handling were memorable but the high-speed ride at low level was certainly bumpier than Tornado. The F-16 trip, from Hahn airfield, also in a two-sticker, was a delight. It was the only side-stick aircraft I have flown and the limited movement of the 'compliant' stick was surprisingly easy to become familiar with. On that sortie I experienced in-flight refuelling from a USAF tanker using the 'boom' system; somewhat scary to have the boom being manoeuvred by the tanker operator over your head while you concentrate on formating on the tanker! It was at Bitburg that we were amused to find two plaques on the corridor wall in the USAF fighter squadron office block. The first stated, 'It's no good simply being *involved* in this squadron, you've got to be *COMMITTED*.' And the second gave the definition of 'committed': 'On your bacon and egg breakfast you'll see that the hen was involved, but the pig was committed.'

In November 1981 we made the first firing of the Skyflash missile, which was to be the ADV's primary weapon. On 12 November, with Les Hurst in the back seat, we carried out the Skyflash jettison trials from ADV A02, ZA267. A week later, with Paul Kelly in the back of the same aircraft, we made the first firing, over Cardigan Bay on the Aberporth range. All previous ADV flying had been carried out with dummy missiles fitted in their semi-submerged positions under the fuselage, and we were finally to feel the clunking of the missile crutch system that pushed the weapon clear of the aircraft before ignition and then thumped back into the belly.

During 1982 and 1983 the pace of Tornado production, both the Strike and the Air Defence Variant, noticeably increased. Deliveries of the Strike version to the TTTE at Cottesmore continued and the prototypes P02 and P06 were involved in development of the -6 engine and gun firing of the Mauser cannon respectively. This latter exercise was a good example of the intricacies of the flight test schedules. In producing a carpet of plots, the

ADV A02 ZA267 completes the first firing of the Skyflash missile at Aberporth range on 19 November 1981.

engineers might require a two-second cannon burst at conditions that were almost impossible to achieve simultaneously. For example, 'fire under 5g, with the engines slam-accelerating, at 350 knots IAS, at 2,000ft and on a safe range compass heading between 270 and 300 degrees.' It might need two or three attempts to achieve each of the points called for.

In November 1983 I finally achieved a boyhood dream, my first trip in a Spitfire. As mentioned earlier, Cliff Rogers, chief test pilot for Rolls-Royce at its Hucknall airfield, had promised me a flight in the company's Mk.XIV, RM689, back in 1971 when I had spent some time there on its F-4 Phantom programme. When I tried to take up his offer earlier, the aircraft was on maintenance and shortly afterwards Rolls-Royce had to be bailed out by the government when it had a major financial problem. Cliff told me that when the assessors came to Hucknall to value the assets, he managed to 'hide' the Spitfire behind a pile of tyres in the hangar and the company was able to avoid its disposal.

Anyhow, it was saved and I was invited down for a trip. The first memorable aspect of its behaviour was on take-off. Even with a light wind on the nose, full left rudder and trim and after careful line up on the centre line, the aircraft hopped crab-like to the right through the early part of the take-off roll. On later trips I learned to have the nose pointing left and to crab down the centre line. Up and away the handling can only be described as delicate. All three controls were very sensitive, with extremely light stick forces and enthusiastic responses. More than any other aircraft, it simply *wanted* to manoeuvre, to pitch and roll and do aerobatics! As with the old Sea Fury, the biggest gauge on the instrument panel seemed to be the turn-and-slip gauge, and for good reason. This sort of flying was back to the days of constant rudder follow up with power changes and manoeuvre inputs. It must have been a real handful to those young men learning to fly it for more serious reasons in the 1940s. I went back to Hucknall for more over the next two years and later I sadly learned that the aircraft was badly damaged at an air show at Woodford in June 1992.

During 1983 and 1984, development of both Tornado models, strike and air defence, carried on at a steady pace. The ADV radar development was showing good results during interception exercises with our Buccaneer and Lightning targets, and our gun carriage aircraft, P06, continued development of the 27mm Mauser cannon, now alongside the latest engine standard.

During 1984, the first RAF Tornado squadron entered a team into the United States Strategic Air Command Bombing and Navigation Competition. The other entrants were the USAF, flying F-111s and the big B-52s, and the Royal Australian Air Force flying F-111s. In November I went

The author with Rolls-Royce Spitfire Mk.XIV RM689 at Hucknall airfield on 17 November 1983.

to Barksdale Air Force Base, Louisiana, to hear the results and attend the awards ceremony. I remember in particular the large hall that the ceremony was held in, with sloped lecture hall seating crammed with about 200 aircrew in their flying gear.

The bombing tasks set had involved complicated navigation tasks to reach long-distance targets and involved night in-flight refuelling. It transpired that the RAF Tornados had made a clean sweep of all the trophies they had been invited to compete for, but before the results were given, the station commander announced from the stage that before the ceremony he had arranged a short entertainment that he thought this audience would enjoy. To appropriate raunchy music, six or seven shapely young ladies swept on to the stage dressed in brightly coloured leotards performing nightclub style bumps and grinds, and were encouraged with wild applause. When they had left, the station commander said, 'I'm sure you'll be interested to know that you've just been watching the entire flight crew of KC-10 tanker Number 12345.'

In December 1984 I drove over to RAF Finningley, where my daughter, Anna, was a member of the University Air Squadron (UAS) and had recently soloed the Bulldog T.1, an RAF side-by-side trainer. She had managed to get permission to fly her dad and I was very proud to watch her handling this sporty machine. Anna had joined the Hull University UAS the previous year and we had suggested that she should do that to gain some brownie points towards a possible career in the RAF Air Traffic Control section. However, shortly after she joined the UAS, the RAF began to take in females for flying training; something the Americans had been doing for several years (Anna, keen to fly, had asked me to question the RAF on when they might do the same, but Air Vice Marshal Ken Hayre, OC 11 Group, offered no hope that it might be soon). But as soon as it was announced, Anna, with another female student, applied and stormed through the training with flying colours. She was part of the Hull UAS team that won the UAS Aerobatic Trophy in 1985 and, thirty years later, she is now a captain on the Boeing 777 fleet with British Airways!

In early 1985, in among continued Tornado development of supersonic engine handling in A01 and further Mauser gun-firing data gathering in P06, I was able to continue my familiarising with other aircraft. At several Farnborough Air Shows I had been impressed with Andy Jones' demos in the BAe Hawk and I went down to Dunsfold in January for a trip with him in the Hawk demonstrator. Andy kept me honest from the back seat and let me do stalls, spins and general handling. It was certainly highly manoeuvrable

The author being taken flying by his daughter, Anna, on 31 December 1984 in a Bulldog T.1 of Hull University Air Squadron.

with lightish stick forces and good view. I was to get involved with the aircraft from my desk in Panavia in 1987 when the USN bought it as its Pensacola-based trainer and identified some shortcomings in its deck-landing suitability. Warton no longer had a test pilot with naval experience and I was involved in meetings to determine fixes.

I went back down to Dunsfold for a long-awaited trip in the two-seat Harrier G-VTOL with an old navy friend, Taylor Scott, in February 1985, when the snow lay thick on the ground. Taylor had been a Sea Vixen pilot in Simon Idiens' Simon's Sircus aerobatic team, which we had joined up with in our Buccaneer Phoenix Five team at the Farnborough Air Show in 1968. Later, Taylor was detached from the navy to serve as Sea Harrier liaison pilot with BAe at Dunsfold in 1977 and in 1979 he left the navy to join the company as a test pilot, continuing his work on the Harrier at Dunsfold. He had been seconded back to the navy briefly at the start of the Falklands War to brief the Sea Harrier crews involved on the Sidewinder AIM-9L missile installation into the Sea Harrier.

Familiarisation with
Hawk G-HAWK
at Dunsfold on
24 January 1985.

The remarkable V/STOL Harrier had been developed from the Hawker Siddeley P.1127 and had been given its first tethered and then conventional flights by Bill Bedford in 1960. I saw a good deal of Bill many years later when we were both elected fellows of the Society of Experimental Test Pilots, and his descriptions of his early adventures with this aircraft were hilarious. Fellow ETPS student John Farley became synonymous with the Harrier in later years and, as well as major contributions to its development, gave superb demonstrations of it around the world. Before I had my trip with Taylor, my daughter Anna, in her guise as a University Air Squadron cadet, had cadged a backseat ride in one from her Boscombe Down summer camp and so at last I was about to catch up with her!

I would like to add here another link with this vertical take-off arrangement. During my time at Boscombe Down in the 1960s I had worked closely in C Squadron with Dennis Higton, who as mentioned earlier had been the chief performance engineer during the carrier suitability trials of the Buccaneer Mk2 aboard the USS *Lexington*. Dennis told me many years later that it was he who, as an apprentice at Farnborough in the 1950s, had been called into his boss's office one day, to be told: 'Higton, Rolls-Royce have just produced a jet engine that produces more thrust than its own weight. It will soon be possible to design an aircraft that can take off vertically. Go away and design a rig that we can use to develop the means of controlling it with no forward speed.' Dennis showed me his notebooks of the day with his first sketches of what became the Flying Bedstead.

Taylor gave me a good briefing on the Harrier. I was interested in the 'threepenny bit' manoeuvring that I had heard about from the Harrier pilots at Yeovilton during my annual naval reserve flying. In one-v-one dog fighting, they claimed to be able to pull the gunsight up on to the target in a tight turn by briefly moving the nozzles down and back again to the conventional flight position, but at the expense of a loss of airspeed. From our snow-covered dispersal we took off in Harrier demonstrator G-VTOL vertically – a huge advantage! Excellent cockpit view and apparently plenty of excess thrust gave a clean break from Mother Earth. I was expecting a noisy environment at low airspeeds but this didn't seem to be the case. Up and away, the conventional handling was very straightforward with lightish stick forces and good response. It was not really possible to assess the threepenny bitting without a target to pull against but certainly any nozzle movement while pulling G inevitably lost speed quite significantly. Back at the airfield I was allowed to do the transition to the hover, initially with white knuckles, and to discover the delights of being purely jet-borne. I had been warned about avoiding excessive yaw rates and eventually relaxed and enjoyed it. I was impressed at how simple the mixing of the two modes of control had been made, the transfer of jet borne to wing borne.

Very sadly, Taylor Scott was killed in a bizarre Harrier accident in October 1987. He had recently been appointed deputy chief test pilot at Dunsfold and was doing a late afternoon test flight in a Harrier GR5. He had climbed to 30,000ft and was heading west over Salisbury Plain when military radar control found he was heading out of his assigned area and was no longer responding to radio calls. Eventually they asked a US Air Force C-5 that was in the area to rendezvous with the aircraft and this crew reported that the aircraft was continuing west, apparently on autopilot, the canopy was missing from the aircraft and there was no pilot on board. His body was found the following day on Salisbury Plain. Apparently the ejection seat drogue gun had fired, dragging him out through the canopy with a torn parachute.

The two-seat Harrier G-VTOL making a ski-jump take-off.

In April that year, 1985, Chris Yeo, then chief test pilot at Warton, and I delivered the last two Nigerian Air Force Jaguars to Makurdi Air Base via Alghero in Sardinia and Tamanrasset in the Algerian Sahara. I recall an exciting formation take-off from the 4,500ft-high Tamanrasset airport in 35°C temperature and with 2 × 1,200-litre tanks. We used every last inch of their runway.

In July 1985, the Warton managing director, Frank Roe, finally took up my offer to give him a trip in a Tornado. We fitted this in with a production test flight of British Strike Aircraft BS153, which had only minor test points to complete before I was able to show Frank the route we had used for our demonstrations to various service and other VIPs. This entailed climbing for a brief squirt to supersonic speeds, descent to the Isle of Man, crossing the Irish Sea to coast in at Whitehaven and then low level using automatic terrain-following to the high ground to the west of Newcastle and Durham, which was the area of Frank's youth. Back at home we overflew the Samlesbury and Preston BAe sites before landing, and he was clearly highly pleased to have been able to experience this most successful product of his BAe team.

In November that year I took P06 on its final retirement trip to RAF Cosford. I had made its first flight just ten years earlier in December 1975 and in those years it had been worked hard, initially on improvements to directional handling and sorting out the optimal shape of the rear fuselage below the fin. We had used it to show MRCA for the first time at Farnborough in 1976 and it had been used to develop the operation of the 27mm Mauser high-velocity cannon. As mentioned, we had flown it as a single seater. RAF Cosford was to use the aircraft for training armourers in loading and unloading the various stores.

On my initial approach to the Cosford runway, the thrust reverser system indicated that one bucket would not have deployed, and since reverse was going to be needed for this short runway I had to take the aircraft back to Warton to get it fixed before being able to finally hand her over.

The following year, 1986, was going to be my last flying from Warton. Our normal retirement age in BAe category 1 test flying was 50. I had already passed that in December 1985 but I continued quietly on as director flight operations, with the firm intention of making the first flight of the Experimental Aircraft Programme (EAP) aircraft, which we were already simulating and which was beginning to take shape in the hangar. On 5 February I took our first British Tornado prototype, the stalwart P02, down to Honington to hand it over to the RAF for use as a ground instruction rig, just over eleven years after its first flight.

In March 1986, with chief navigator George McCauley in the back seat, we took the first four Tornados to our new customer, the Royal Saudi Air Force.

Chief navigator George McCauley helps Warton's M.D. Frank Roe into Tornado BS153 on 23 July 1985.

The first four Royal Saudi Air Force Tornados preparing to leave Warton on 26 March 1986.

BAe's contracts director, Maurice Dixon, full of confidence some three months before, had promised the Saudis the Tornados would be delivered to Dharan during a planned air show there, at something like 8.30 a.m. local time on 27 March. This we achieved by flying into Akrotiri, Cyprus, the night before and departing very early. The superbly accurate Tornado navigation system allowed us to arrive at the Saudi air display right on the planned time after a three-hour forty-minute flight and the delivery crews were royally entertained at an unforgettable welcoming dinner that evening.

In July 1986, we flew our first example of the TERPROM system, the name being derived from terrain profile matching. A BAe-designed system, it consisted of a bubble memory that could be loaded into the navigational software, with three-dimensional map data to provide the equivalent of our Tornado radar-derived terrain following information and continuous present position. Tornado P12 was modified to carry it for research. We followed the flight director dot in the head-up display and it effectively gave terrain following commands without the detectable external transmissions using the standard radar version. I felt somewhat sceptical initially at the thought of contour following at night with no forward-looking sensor, but this was the developing technology!

8

EAP

During April, activities around the Experimental Aircraft Programme (EAP) aircraft began to dominate my time. The aircraft was close to completion, the engines were fitted and engine running was started in the engine bay on the south side of Warton airfield. As well as looking at the basic engine response and the fuel system capabilities, we were looking at possible interaction of intake flow through the common chin intake with the two engines at dissimilar power settings. There were no problems.

The layout of the EAP was the result of about ten years' work. The design office had worked through a P106, referred to as the single engine Light Combat Aircraft (LCA), with a cranked delta wing, and the P110, a larger twin-engine fighter. Both had canards and both were flown on the flexible Warton simulator doing parametric comparisons with various other 'paper' aircraft. Through the same period, MBB had also been researching similar unstable layouts and the two got together with the third Tornado partner, Aeritalia, and proposed the European Combat Aircraft (ECA). They attempted to get the French to join the programme but as usual, I believe, the French wanted to lead the design and so discussions were continued in 1982 with only BAe, MBB and Aeritalia. At the 1982 Farnborough Air Show a joint proposal of an Agile Combat Aircraft (ACA) was shown as a mock-up and government support was announced for a demonstrator called the EAP. It was intended originally to produce three copies – one in each country – but first the German government and then the Italian government withdrew their support, the Germans being said to feel they were being pressurised by industry. A work-sharing arrangement between the three companies collapsed and BAe alone, with the support of the UK government, went ahead with a very ambitious plan to complete the design, build and first flight of the aircraft within three years. The company did this with a remarkable plan to enlist help from the British aircraft industry, and similar industries in Germany and Italy. Thirty-eight suppliers in the UK and many from Germany and Italy signed up to support the programme at their own expense and the aircraft eventually flew on time and within budget. Aeritalia itself made the left wing and MBB kept a small contribution to remain in the programme. The Tornado engine company Turbo-Union contributed the engines, Mk 104 RB199s as fitted to the Tornado ADV, but with thrust reversers removed and some other minor simplification.

The original work-sharing plans had included the centre fuselage and fin being manufactured by MBB using new technologies but when the German government withdrew support, BAe was forced to redesign these areas and adopt some Tornado methods and parts to stay on programme. Nevertheless, new advanced structures and materials were used in other parts of the airframe and this remained one of the primary objectives in this programme, in particular CFRP (carbon fibre reinforced plastics). BAe had already established a carbon fibre facility at its Samlesbury factory, the former home of Canberra and Lightning construction. The other objectives were to achieve an aerodynamic design giving carefree handling to a high angle of attack with a highly unstable configuration; to demonstrate active control technology; to demonstrate a digital data bus control of the avionic system; and to produce a modern cockpit design.

And now, in the spring of 1986, as well as engine running, the various EAP systems were being exercised and meetings with the flight test department

The EAP at Warton in October 1985. Note the CFRP skin on wing, foreplane and forward fuselage.

were held to map out what we might do on the early flights. I could not see why we should not try to get supersonic on the first flight and we made that an aim, assuming, of course, there were no unexpected problems.

On an EAP simulator a very accurate flying control software simulation was being slowly developed, in which test pilot Pete Orme, now designated EAP project pilot, was heavily involved. BAe at Warton had developed a strong expertise in this area and had assisted Saab in the flying control design of its relaxed stability JAS 39 Gripen fighter.

Then, in late July, EAP was finally ready for its taxi tests and high-speed runs. The first slow taxi tests showed that the nosewheel steering was too sensitive: too highly geared. After a two-day delay to tweak the relevant software we moved on to fast taxi runs to lift-off speeds. These tests were made fully strapped in and with ejection seat armed, and with flight test engineer Dave Ward and his team orchestrating the operation from the desk of the telemetry room. The reaction of the flying controls to the normal nodding in pitch as the aircraft taxied was made very obvious by the foreplane, which bounced about enthusiastically. To confirm tailplane power and flying control reaction I set the aircraft up as for take-off, to accelerate to around 120 knots, raise the nose, chop the power and select tailchute to decelerate.

The first surprise was that the aircraft would not hold even close to full dry power on the brakes, but slid forward on locked brakes. The all-up weight was just short of 17,000kg and the RB199s were to the Mk 104 standard as in the Tornado ADV, so they were producing around 9,000lb thrust each in just dry power (reheat unlit). That made the power-to-weight ratio significantly better than Tornado. So final checks were done at about 90 per cent dry power before slamming to max reheat and releasing the brakes. Acceleration was impressive and pitch control was crisp and stable. Everything felt good, though on chopping the power the brake chute took some two to three seconds to produce its effect, which seemed sluggish when everything else about the operation seemed to be effective immediately. Selecting 'lift dump' after the derotation moved the foreplanes to their 'barn door' braking position but with no obvious increase in deceleration at this low airspeed. After three repeats of this accel/decel exercise the flight test engineers retired to confirm that the recorded data matched prediction.

The aircraft was ready for its first flight two days later but the weather then reduced to 'gloomy'. Normal operations and test flying of other types continued but conditions were not suitable for the first flight of a new type. After a remarkable record of keeping to a very tight build programme, the frustrations of the whole team were very obvious as the aircraft was pulled out each morning for three days and later put back into the hangar, still cold. But on 8 August the visibility improved enough to go by early afternoon (see colour plate 28).

During my flying time with BAe I had kept up my allegiance to the Fleet Air Arm by toting the 'Fly Navy' logo wherever possible and during the wait for weather I asked the paint shop to add it to what we all hoped was to be the demonstrator for a new fighter for the Royal Air Force. A question about political correctness apparently got back to Frank Roe, who simply said. 'If that's what he wants you'd better do it!'

The first flight schedule was simple and straightforward. We planned to exercise the landing gear, check the general handling at 10,000, 20,000 and 30,000ft, take the aircraft supersonic to Mach 1.1 if all was well and look at slow speed handling and handling in the circuit. And that's the way it went (see Experimental Flight Report at Appendix 4). The aircraft was strongly attitude stable and yet very responsive to control input, a very desirable combination. Stick forces in pitch were slightly heavier than our classic British standard as seen in the 'yardstick' Hunter. In roll they were also slightly heavier, but in both axes forces were, in my view, ideal considering the response being generated. There was a slight rumbling from the cockpit floor when the engines were throttled back sharply, obviously intake spillage, and slight noise from the foreplane jack when an abrupt pitch input was made. Overall though, it was smooth, quiet and a delight to handle, even though the leading edge flaps, which were to be an active part of the flying control system, were locked for the early flying. It would obviously have made a superb fighter as it stood, with the introduction of a weapons system. From the cockpit point of view the limited displacement stick took no getting used to. During the design phase we had discussed the optimum degree of seat recline angle and whether we should go for a side stick like the F-16. To avoid loss of right console panel space we chose a centre stick but with limited displacement. The displays were very familiar after hours of staring at them during ground engine running time, and it was good to confirm that up in the bright sunlight at high altitude they kept their colour well and remained easily readable (see colour plate 29).

We had hoped the EAP could be shown to the public at the Farnborough Air Show that year and I had proposed that Chris Yeo, then chief test pilot at Warton, should fly it. When the first flight went so well, with the only snags all being fully understood and acceptable for immediate further flight, we

The EAP cockpit layout.

kept the programme running with Farnborough in mind. Both Chris and I flew it again two days later and Pete Orme was invited to take flight five. I should add that in earlier days it was expected that with a completely new aircraft type, flying would be very much restricted to one or two pilots at the most until experience and confidence in all aspects of its handling had been built up. EAP from the beginning showed a reliability and ease of handling that allowed confident sharing of its early revelations (see colour plate 30).

Chris worked up a gentle routine for Farnborough and gave the aircraft its first public airing at the air show on its twenty-eighth flight on 31 August 1986, and repeated it on each of the next seven days. It was an excellent, confident and outstanding start to a programme that was to make significant contributions to the Typhoon, the fighter that was the original objective of the Experimental Aircraft Programme (see colour plate 31).

9

Shut Down

My final couple of months' flying at Warton included some fuel tank jettison trials from the strike Tornado and radar assessment sorties in the third prototype ADV. We also had a need to do an air test on the Warton two-seat Hunter XL586, which we used for chase duties, and which had shown problems with the oxygen system at altitude. So I had an empty seat and was able to invite my son, Simon, who was working at BAe under the apprentice scheme, to fly with me for the one and only time. Unfortunately the weather was lousy so he didn't get to see much from the air.

My last flight before retirement from Warton was a production test on Tornado ADV AT17, with Roy Kenward in the back seat. After completing the schedule I asked to make a low pass past flight operations and aimed to run by at about Mach 0.95 to celebrate completion. Unfortunately I was a touch fast and we had complaints of excessive noise and some light damage from a dweller in the caravan park on the airfield boundary. I was highly embarrassed at the time because I had always kept a firm hand on such over-enthusiasm and was very unhappy to leave with a complaint in Chris Yeo's in-tray. Some years later, after I had retired to New Zealand, we had a visit from Tony Baxter, who had been the managing director at Warton at that time. With a smile on his face he brought with him a 'bill' for the damage that that fly-by had caused.

Having formally retired on my 51st birthday in December 1986, and while arrangements were being made for me to take up the appointment of Deputy Managing Director of Panavia in Munich, I was finally able to take up the promise of some trips in Spitfire PR Mk XIX PS915, which had been restored back to flying condition by British Aerospace at Samlesbury. The aircraft was a photo reconnaissance version of the Spitfire with a Rolls-Royce Griffon 58 series engine and its restoration was a gift from BAe to the RAF Battle of Britain Memorial Flight. It had previously been the gate guardian at RAF Brawdy and had been dismantled and taken by road to Samlesbury in

The author with his son,
Simon, and Hunter XL586
at Warton on 14 November
1986.

June 1984 (my memories of Brawdy were of a visit to the then RNAS Brawdy
with 893 Squadron Sea Venoms, for gunnery and rocketing practice in 1959).

Some time back in 1985 I had a look at progress on the restoration and
met Air Commodore Ken Hayre, then AOC Strike Command, to ask if
I could give all my Warton pilots a sortie in the aircraft before it was delivered.
Ken sensibly agreed that only the pilots who had some tailwheel time could
have a trip, though in the end only Keith Hartley, Peter Gordon-Johnson and
myself took up the offer (see colour plate 32).

I have described my impressions of flying the Spitfire earlier in this book
and the delight in being able to fly it gently around the Warton airspace
I knew so well is still live in my memory. It was demanding on take-off
and landing and pure enjoyment when chasing clouds. It was wonderful to
experience after the complication and brutality of the fast jets and pretty
awe-inspiring when you remember that young 19- and 20-year-olds were
fighting for their lives in them in the Second World War.

After spending five years in Munich with Panavia and before retiring to
Tauranga in New Zealand in 1993, I took a flying instructor course at the
BAe College in Prestwick flying the Piper Cherokee and the Piper Seneca.
I did a little instructing at the Tauranga Aero Club in 1995 but eventually

took up gliding with the Tauranga Gliding Club instead, which seemed a much more appropriate pastime for retirement.

In early 1996, and while in the middle of the sticky exercise of honey extracting in the garage at our home in New Zealand, I had a telephone call from Herr Rauen in Munich. I had known Ays since my Panavia days; he had been the Tornado project manager for MBB and risen quickly in the company. He had recently been made managing director and was asking if I would go back to Germany to run the flight test directorate for three years. I was flattered but reluctant to put my enjoyable retirement on hold for that length of time; eventually I agreed to go back for a year. In April I moved into a small appartment in Fuchsbuchlerstrasse, Guisenfeld, which was a small village immediately next to the German government airfield of Manching, 100km north of Munich. The German government had its military flight test base there and MBB had had a lodger unit there, containing its own flight test directorate, for many years. The company's main design and engineering centre was in Ottobrun, Munich.

The ongoing programmes at Manching when I arrived in April 1996 included the Eurofighter (later to be called Typhoon) first prototype, which had made its maiden flight here two years earlier. The development programme was making slow progress, with British and Italian prototypes already involved and a Spanish two-seat trainer about to fly. The Tornado programme was also providing work still, mainly related to weapon and attack system developments. And Manching also had an ex-East German Air Force Mig 29, which the chief test pilot, Wolfgang Schirdewahn, demonstrated with some panache.

My year there was full and varied and pretty challenging. I found the industrial relations aspects in Germany so very different from those in the UK. At Warton the test pilots and engineers worked at whatever hours the project required to get the job done. In Manching, if a test pilot went to an engineering meeting at Ottobrun, he would leave that meeting with enough time to drive back to Manching to finish at 5 p.m., as his contract dictated. I spent some time encouraging the pilots to get involved in the earliest stages of design, and in encouraging the heads of department to involve them, as was the practice at Warton (see Appendix 6).

One very memorable event during my time at Manching was a visit in December 1996 to the Russian test pilot school at the Gromov Institute at Zhukovsky near Moscow. My efforts to recruit a new test pilot had been neutered by a German law that prevented the company giving a job to a member of the forces for five years after he left the service. This was obviously a sound move with the intention of preventing a serviceman with necessary close contact to industry from building up an unhealthily close relationship before leaving in order to secure a position. But in the case of test pilots, their value to a company is largely based on their being in current practice. And a fast-jet test pilot leaving the service is anyway likely to be of an age when he will not have many more useful years ahead of him at the job. We got as far as meetings with the Minister of Defence trying to have this rule bypassed in the case of test pilots but to no avail. So we announced that we would look at employing a graduate of the Russian test pilot school, largely in the hope that this would lead to a change of mind. And through the German Embassy in Moscow (which would obviously keep Bonn informed) we formally requested a visit to Zhukovsky. Our visit, in November 1996, was led by a retired ex-West German general from the Konrad Adenauer Institute in Bonn, who had many contacts in Russia. In Moscow we met Anatoly Markusha and Col Smirnov, both ex-test pilots of note, and they came with us to the school.

We took an hour's trip by road, through the grim suburbs of Moscow, past miles of massive accommodation blocks that all showed terrible signs of disrepair. There was missing stonework and window frames, curtains, if any, nailed over windows, muddy ground between them and everywhere the look of a building site not yet finished yet obviously untouched for years. The guardhouse of the Gromov Flight Research Institute at Zhukovsky looked equally ugly and uncared for. We were shown through an apparently deserted military base to the test pilots' school, where we walked up two flights of stairs, crunching fallen plaster underfoot, to the office of Honoured Test Pilot Vladimir Kodratenko, chief of the test pilot school. We spoke to him for an hour or so through his female English language teacher, who also spoke good German. He had four students on the current ten-month course who were all funded by one of the major companies, Mikoyan, Sukhoi, Ilyushin, etc. The school was not funded in any way by the government; it had to cover all costs from the companies' payments. We learned about the qualifications required to take the course, the number of types and hours flown by the students and the syllabus they followed.

After lunch of red cabbage soup, a bitter cabbage salad and a strange piece of meat, came the saddest experience of all. Kodratenko asked if we would like to take a drive over the airfield to see the aircraft parked there. On the enormous field were several huge development bureaus belonging to the big companies, each with a large hangar, an engineering block and an enormous hardstanding – about five in all. On the hardstandings were a total of around

200 aircraft, apparently abandoned. There were prototypes of every Russian aircraft you have ever seen pictured. There were two Concordskis, enormous variable sweep bombers and huge missile carriers. The Buran Space Shuttle was there, with three or four jet engines fixed at the rear with which it had flown from this airfield for handling trials. It looked very similar to the American Space Shuttle, which of course was taken airborne piggy back on a Boeing 747 and released at altitude as a means of getting it into the air for its handling trials. There were fighters, trainers, eight or ten of each type, the navy's vertical take-off fighter, strange jet bombers with wheels at the wing tips as well as bogies beneath, and a bomber converted to carry the Buran. There were airliners with engines unblanked, continually windmilling in the strong breeze, apparently forever. It was a collection of the most fascinating technology, all abandoned and left to rot with grass growing through the asphalt around the wheels, engines hanging off and few with any kind of covers. There were about six to seven AWACS types with enormous disc-shaped covered aerials mounted on top, all peeling. It was like one enormous museum, or rather mausoleum. And the tragedy was, of course, that the unbelievable cost of the industry that had produced all this was the element missing from the houses, roads, apartments and pensions throughout Russia. I came away with a huge sorrow for these people who had slaved away to produce this wealth of technology, for little reward, and who now saw the whole thing thrown away and yet had no obvious improvement in their prospects. This was 1996, seven years after the fall of the Berlin Wall.

The people we met were all very honest about their lot and very bitter. It was almost embarassing to talk about our own lives when anything you could mention was an unbelievable luxury to them. We had taken the usual handouts to thank them for letting us see the school, and one of our number had taken tins of food for Smirnov and the Markushas. We heard endlessly of the corruption throughout the new establishment and the terrible state of the army and air force life. An open letter in the current Russian Air Force monthly paper, from the wife of an air force pilot officer, said that she thought that they didn't need the extra fuel (which obviously the previous edition had called for) – all she longed for was was to be given a flat where she didn't have to stay awake all night to make sure the rats didn't eat her baby.

My enjoyable time back in Europe with Daimler-Benz Aerospace (later called DASA) finished in April 1996 and I went back to my beekeeping in New Zealand. Six years later I divorced and returned to the UK and in 2008 I married Ann Kendal-Ward, in Oxfordshire, and lived happily ever after.

Appendix 1

ETPS No. 22 Fixed Wing Course, Final Exam Paper (page 1), Farnborough, October 1963.

EMPIRE TEST PILOTS' SCHOOL

NO. 22 FIXED WING COURSE

FINAL EXAMINATION (TECHNICAL)

MONDAY 28TH OCTOBER, 1963

Attempt any FIVE questions

Time allowed – 3 hours

Books A, B, and C, and the A. & A.E.E. Technical Guide may be used.

1. (a) The methods used in the reduction of the flight test results of jet engine aircraft are based on a non-dimensional analysis of the airframe and engine performance. What are the advantages and disadvantages of this non-dimensional approach?

(b) Show that the level speed performance of a jet aircraft can be represented by a relationship of the form:

$$M = f\left(\frac{N}{\sqrt{\theta}}, \frac{W}{p}\right)$$

(Do not, however, go into the detailed dimensional analysis of this problem).

2. The specific air range characteristics of a particular aircraft are shown in non-dimensional form in Fig.6 of Chapter B/9.

Determine the maximum value of the specific air range that can be achieved, when the aircraft is flying at a pressure height of 42,000 ft, with an A.U.W. of 25,000 lb. What are the corresponding values of the airspeed (E.A.S.), the Mach number, and the engine R.P.M., required to obtain the optimum S.A.R., in standard atmospheric conditions? The minimum drag speed (E.A.S.) of the aircraft is given by $V_{i_{md}} = 0.9107 \sqrt{W}$ kts.

3. The methods of reduction used for the results obtained from the jet aircraft ceiling climb and slow climb cruise flight tests both contain differential corrections involving changes of engine R.P.M.

(a) Discuss this particular aspect of these two reduction processes, explaining in your own words:

(i) why these corrections are necessary

and (ii) how the corrections are made.

(b) What additional information has to be known, or determined, to enable this particular section of each of these reductions to be completed?

4. (a) Show that a rotating vector and a sine wave can be used as alternative representations of an undamped oscillatory motion.

(b) Draw the time-vector diagram of the forces acting in a spring-mass-viscous damper system. Why has the diagram got the particular shape that you have shown?

/(c)

Page one of the ETPS No. 22 Fixed Wing Course final exam paper, at Farnborough in October 1963.

Appendix 2

Typical Flight Test Report, C Squadron, Boscombe Down, January 1966.

A typical four-page flight test report at C Squadron, Boscombe Down in January 1966.

DRAFT

From:- Lt.Cdr.J.D.Eagles,R.N.

To:- The Commanding Officer,
"C" Squadron

Date:-

Ref:- AFW36/038

Copies to:-

Superintendent of Flying
Superintendent of Performance
Superintendent of Engineering
Superintendent of W.S.Div.
Superintendent of Nav.Radio
Superintendent of Armament
C.C.Handling Squadron

"C" Perf Tech Section
"C" Eng Tech Section

Sea Vixen FAW Mk.2, XN.685
Flight Refuelling from Argosy C.Mk.1., XN.814

1. **Introduction**

A feasibility study was carried out at A. & A.E.E., into the use of the Argosy aircraft as an in-flight refuelling tanker. Since this study could result in a retrospective C.A. Release for the use of this aircraft in the flight refuelling role, the opportunity was taken to carry out a test to determine the behaviour of Sea Vixen XN.685, while refuelling from the Argosy.

2. **Conditions Relevant to the Test**

2.1. **Condition of the Tanker**

Argosy C.Mk.1, XN.814 was a standard production model, except that a Mk.20D Flight Refuelling Pod was fitted externally on the lower port side, aft on the fuselage.

2.2. **Condition of Sea Vixen XN.685**

Sea Vixen XN.685 was an aerodynamically standard Mk.II model, and carried no stores. The aircraft's fuel system was internally incomplete to the extent that fuel could not be received through the Flight Refuelling Probe. The Probe itself, however, was standard.

2.3. **Weather, Time and Place**

One sortie was flown from A. & A.E.E. on 19th January, 1966. The weather was cloud-free and smooth at test height.

2.4. **Limitations**

2.4.1. **Tanker Limitations**

Tanker limitations which were relevant were as follows:-

V.N.E.   270 E.A.S.

Max.permitted speed with
Refuelling Drogue streamed:- 205 E.A.S.

2.4.2. **Receiver Limitations**

Sea Vixen limitations which were relevant were as follows:-

Max. I.A.S. with half flap:-   220knots.

2.5. **Weight and C.G.**

The following Sea Vixen weight and C.G. details applied:-

Max.permitted A.U.W.	45,700lbs
Permissible C.G.Range	7.60" to 22.20" A.O.D.
A.U.W. at take-off	39,872lbs
C.G. at take-off	11.94" A.O.D.

2.6. **Pilot's Experience**

The pilot's experience included 620 hours in Sea Vixen aircraft including approximately 50 flight refuelling contacts.

2.7. **Photographic Coverage**

All contacts were covered by hand-held cine from a Meteor chase aircraft.

Tests Made

3.1. **Flight Refuelling Dry Contacts at 5,000feet**

Results of Tests

4.1. **Flight Refuelling Dry Contacts at 5,000feet**

The Argosy Tanker streamed its Mk.20D drogue at 5,000ft. at its maximum permissible streaming speed of 205 knots E.A.S. When the Sea Vixen was moved in behind the drogue it was noted that there was a complete absence of slipstream effect from the Tanker and consequently no out-of-trim effect on the Sea Vixen. The Sea Vixen was flown up to 15 feet above and below the trailing drogue, between the contact position and 50feet astern, and nowhere within that region was any slipstream noted. When the Sea Vixen was flown more than 15 feet above the drogue, a light buffeting was felt on the tailplane.

To make contact the Sea Vixen was flown with the probe approximately 6 feet behind, and level with, the drogue. Since the Argosy's drogue was offset a similar distance from the centre line to the offset of the probe from the pilot's cockpit of the Sea Vixen, this resulted in the Vixen pilot being exactly lined up in azimuth with the easily discernible centre line of the Argosy's fuselage. Power was then applied to give approximately 5 knots overtaking speed. There was no apparent drogue movement due to interference from the Sea Vixen, and since there was no turbulence experienced, no control movements were required during the approach. Fuel state at the start of the first approach was 5,200lbs (A.U.W.34,768lbs), and flap was not used, and the tailplane angle was approximately 1.9 degrees nose up. The normal Sea Vixen technique was used in that once an approach had been started from the position 6 feet astern, further control movements were kept to a minimum and the pilot kept his eyes on an aiming mark on the tanker until he saw in appeared that these contacts where the probe struck the inside of the basket first, before moving into the centre did not result in a normal lock.

5. Conclusions

The lack of slipstream effect from the Argosy tanker was no doubt the main reason for the ease with which the Sea Vixen could be plugged in at such comparartively low speeds.

It was felt that the tests demonstrated that the Sea Vixen Mk.2 (and by anology the Mk.1) could safely be brought into contact with the Argosy's drogue under the conditions set down in paragraph 4.1. The Argosy is able to make an E.A.S. of 205 knots up to a maximum altitude of approximately 19,000feet. It is considered that there will be no difference in handling while ¤ntacting the drogue between the test height of 5,000feet and ,000feet.

Thus it is felt that a Release could safely be given the Service to carry out flight refuelling with the Argosy ʘker at E₁A.S.'s between 190 and 205 knots up to 10,000feet. ̄ half flap case gave most control and a higher C.L. to cater ˙ higher A.U.W.s. The effect of increasing the Sea Vixen's ̣W. to maximum (46,000lbs) by flight refuelling at such a ̄paratively low I.A.S. must be considered, but it is felt that ̣cient "G" margin before the stall remains in hand under these ̣itions for the sort of manoeuvring required.

̄over
Recommendations

It is recommended that, should the Argosy Tanker come ‍Service, a C.A. Release should be issued to permit the Sea ̄s F.A.W.1 and F.A.W.2. to refuel from the Argosy by day, in the following limitations:-

Configuration:-	Half Flap
Speed:-	190 to 205knots E.A.S.
Height:-	Any height at which an Argosy can achieve an E.A.S.of 190 to 205knots.

It is recommended that, should the Argosy Tanker come into ʘce, further trials should be carried out to investigate the ̣g of a Release for refuelling at night.

J.D.Eagle

(J.D.Eagles)
Lieutenant Commander RN

his peripheral vision that he was just short of contact. He then watched the drogue and noted the amount and direction of his error if he missed contact. During the test, three approaches out of five resulted in contact.

It was expected that tailplane response might be a limiting factor during refuelling at such a comparatively low airspeed. When first positioning behind the Tanker and when positioning the probe accurately behind the drogue in elevation, tailplane response was indeed noted to be slightly low, but in no way limiting. Once in position the stability of the Vixen in pitch, the complete lack of slipstream effect from the Tanker and the high degree of stability of the drogue all resulted in an exceptionally stable approach.

Two approaches were made during which coarse tailplane movements were used to correct the line-up in elevation. The fuel states during these approaches were 4,750lbs (A.U.W.34,318lbs) and 4,450lbs(A.U.W.34,018lbs). The slightly low tailplane response (compared to the response at the more usual refuelling I.A.S. of 250knots) was noticeable but not limiting and led to no adverse handling features.

Altogether, eight approaches, resulting in five contacts were made in the flapless configuration, at A.U.W.s between 34,768lbs and 34,018lbs at an E.A.S. of 205 knots.

At the same E.A.S. of 205 knots and at an A.U.W. of 33,818lbs, three more approaches (two contacts) were made using half flap. The aircraft attitude was reduced by an estimated five degrees and tailplane response slightly improved. The approaches and contacts were again straight-forward and although the improvement in tailplane response was clearly noted, the task was not felt to be any easier because of it.

In the same configuration of half flap, two contacts were then made at an E.A.S. of 195 knots and two at 185kts. There was no noticeable difference when approaches were made at 195knots, and at 185knots, only a slight reduction in tailplane response was noted which did not make contact any more difficult. Fuel states during these approaches were 3,500lbs (A.U.W.33,068lbs) at 195knots and 3,150lbs(A.U.W. 32,718lbs) at 185knots.

Although fuel was not taken on during the test, the hose was reeled in to the normal refuelling position on each contact. When breaking contact it was noted that on very few of the contacts had the probe locked correctly into the drogue. On only three of the withdrawals did the hose stretch and spring off positively as the probe left the basket. These three contacts had all been apparently "hard" with the probe striking close to, or on, the centre of the drogue. It

Appendix 3

Air Force Magazine, June 1980
Air Force Association, Washington DC

'Flying an 800-Knot Tornado'

A Pilot Report

The need to stay fast and low these days is obvious to all strike pilots. The higher you fly, the more likely ground-to-air weapons are to pick you off, and this is true even when you're using defensive electronic countermeasures. The ability to stay down at 200 feet even at night or in our famous European "murk" is invaluable. And the Tornado is the first aircraft produced in Europe that has that capability. Let me tell you more about it.

While you do the walkaround, your navigator settles into the back seat and starts his inertial navigation system (IN) alignment. There are no ground power or starter trucks on the line. The aircraft auxiliary power unit (APU) is already running and powering the right-hand generator and hydraulic pump. The APU uses aircraft fuel and is designed to power up the aircraft on standby for four hours. As you walk around the aircraft, you'll by surprised at its small size, and that's another aid to survival in the low-level attack game. Its empty weight is around 30,000 pounds, but it is densely packed and has about the same surface area as the F-18. For today's mission the aircraft is carrying eight 1,000-pound bombs under the fuselage, and the wing stations are empty.

Into the cockpit and strap in. The Martin Baker Mk. 10 seat is comfortable and quick to strap into even though it has the addition of arm restraint cords to attach. With a normal operating regime of very high indicated airspeeds, the air forces that will be using the Tornado specified some tight survival requirements.

Arm flailing would be inevitable at ejection speeds, above 500 knots indicated airspeed (IAS), without restraint.

One thing that large and slightly ungainly nose has provided is a wide roomy cockpit, and after the cockpits of the B A C Lightning and British/French Jaguar fighters, this one looks like a ballroom. The size of the nose radome itself was dictated by the dimensions and layout of the two antennas for the Ground-Mapper and the Terrain-Following (TF) radars, the first of which the navigator is checking now with its Built-In Test Equipment (BITE). Cockpit layout in the front is pretty conventional, dominated by the big five-inch lens Head-Up Display (HUD) and the Head-Down Repeater Projected Map Display in the center. Other features that might be new to you, depending on your background, are the "E" Scope high up on the left front panel, which will give you raw returns from the Texas Instruments TF radar, and the hand controller – a small handle just behind the throttles with various switches, enabling the pilot to control some of the HUD attack symbology and thus input to the aircraft's main computer.

I'm going to pause here to add that the cockpit layout is a remarkable achievement of agreement among four air forces (German Air Force, German Navy, Italian Air Force and Royal Air Force). You can almost guarantee as many opinions as there are pilots involved when you discuss cockpit matters, and in this case we had graduates from all four of the Western test pilot schools; i.e., USAF TPS, USN TPS, the French TPS, and the Empire Test Pilot's School. The result of their efforts works really well. The only difference between layouts in aircraft for the different air forces is that some government-furnished equipment boxes were specified individually; e.g., radio and information friend or foe (IFF) controllers have different layouts, but are in the same relative position in the cockpits.

If you had paused to look into the back cockpit on your way to your seat, you would have seen a much greater change from convention. The same roomy cockpit space has allowed a logical panel layout, but the front panel at eye level, is all electronic with a Combined Radar and Projected Map Display flanked by two TV Tabular Displays and associated keyboards. The radar hand controller sits on a pedestal between the operator's knees, and the TV Tabs allow dialogue with the computer, which stores 65,000 bits of information in its memory.

Why two seats? That debate is endless. I believe that with high-speed, low-level bombing, the probability of mission success is much improved by splitting the workload. Of course, the single-seat solution CAN be mechanized – the early Tornado investigations did it – but the result is very much less flexible than the two-seat version. It is easy, for example, to successfully fly a single-seat Auto TF laydown bombing attack through weather to take out a planned target. But if another type of target is spotted on the way, if a change of target is ordered while en route, if an evading diversion from planned track is made necessary preventing planned navigation updating, if a single failure occurs necessitating manual instead of Auto Terrain Following – in any of these not unusual cases you would be glad to have someone to share the extra workload while you keep the aircraft out of the weeds.

As you close the canopy for start-up, you will notice with satisfaction the thickness of the windscreen and canopy transparencies and their supporting ironmongery. Weight saving is all right in its place, but on an aircraft that has already demonstrated 800 knots indicated airspeed, and which normally operates well below the maximum ceiling of your average house-sparrow, let's give the crew the necessary protection.

Start-up is simple. The APU is already running the right gearbox, so pressing the starter switch to "Right" simply clutches in the engine to its own gearbox. The two engine gearboxes can be connected via a cross-drive shaft, and in the case of loss of either engine in the air, the cross-drive clutch closes automatically and thus no services are lost from the failed engine. By use of the cross-drive clutch, either engine can be started first from the APU.

The cockpit, with climate conditioning on or off, is quiet. Crew communication problems in the Hawker Siddeley Buccaneer, flying at high speeds, focused attention on this aspect of Tornado. Researchers at the Royal Aircraft Establishment, Farnborough, attached microphone/recorder packs to the development crews during the early high IAS sorties to determine the depth of the "problem". They came back several times because they were having trouble with their kit; noise levels were hardly high enough to register. But that's the way it is. Cockpit noise levels in Tornado at 800 knots are remarkably low and certainly do not affect crew chat levels.

Preflight checks take up very little time. Most systems, including the fly-by-wire Command & Stability Augmentation System (CSAS) and the associated autopilot, have their own BITE, and the only "extra" check on Tornado is to sweep the wing once each way before starting to taxi. Nosewheel steering is permanently engaged, but can be cut out on the stick paddle switch in case of malfunction. In its normal mode, nosewheel steering has a two-slope gearing suitable for take-off, landing, and normal taxiing. For tight turning in a restricted space, a "High" gear can be selected by pressing the "Steering

Engaged" light. Rudder pedal forces are a little higher than optimum for ground handling, but nothing to get worked up about.

While taxiing, we can check on Bob Newhart's "other way of stopping" – i.e., throwing it into reverse! Rocking both throttle levers left through an over-center action spring selects both sets of spoilers to the Lift Dump mode and deploys the engine thrust reverser buckets on whatever engine power is selected at the time. The throttles can continue to be used in the normal way with the reversers deployed; in other words, moving throttles forward increases reverse thrust. So even a failure of both wheel-braking systems wouldn't prevent us from stopping, and we can slow or stop on ice without directional problem – another bonus in Europe.

Running up the Turbo-Union RB.199 engines against the brakes prior to takeoff shows the rapid wind-up times that the electronic control system provides. The link from throttle to engine is all electronic and gives the nicest control that this pilot, anyway, has ever found. You can slam from idle to combat power anywhere in the flight envelope, and it is also possible to very quickly set up a particular engine speed absolutely accurately – a function of rapid response, gauges that can be read to 0.1 percent, and a total lack of creep or sponginess. But the real beauty of these small three-spool fan engines is about to be revealed to us when we get the machine into the air. The RB.199 has the highest thrust-to-volume ratio of any turbine engine in the world today, giving the Tornado a Mach 2+ level flight capability with engines small enough to look at home on a business jet.

Max dry power is held against the toe brakes, then minimum reheat, and finally the throttles are slammed to full combat power as the brakes are released. Acceleration with eight 1,000-pound bombs is good, and the aircraft is lifted off in about half our 6,000-foot runway.

When the flaps are raised from their mid, 35 degree position, they retract only to the "Maneuver" setting of 7 degrees flap, 11 degrees slat. Thereafter, the wing will clean up automatically as incidence is reduced for cruising. With Maneuver extended, we can maintain very high turn rates at sea level, and we are not going to be much above that level during the first part of this sortie.

With the flap/slat retracted, we settle down at the best range speed to fly to the target range and deliver our payload. Normally we would simply put the autopilot on "Trackhold" and let the automatic flight plan take us there. We can choose a pitch channel controlled by either the Terrain-Following Radar or Barometric Height Hold or Radar Height Hold, depending on the desired altitude, and monitor the route on the Projected Map (front seat) and radar in the rear. Fuel flow is back to a very low figure, even with our eight 1,000-pound bombs, and the navigator will plan to update the nav. system twice or three times during the first half hour to guarantee the kind of system accuracy that is going to be required if the weather is poor and we have to lay down the bombs blind. Updating is done by radar and laser ranging, and in visual conditions the pilot can switch into the loop using the fixing marker in the HUD.

But today let us look at aircraft handling on the way to the range.

Pulling the aircraft into a turn at our 350 knots transit speed automatically extends maneuver devices (flap and slat), giving no trim change, but reverting the aircraft from a high wing loading maximum range machine into a lower wing loading, highly maneuverable ship. Stick forces are light to moderate – perhaps slightly lighter than American fashion – and harmony between pitch and roll is excellent. The triplex fly-by-wire system provides superb stability and response, making the aircraft a joy to fly clean or with a heavy payload, at sea level or at 30,000 feet, at 140 knots or at 800 knots. As an example of control-system performance, full stick roll rate is identical between zero and four "G" in 25 degrees, 45 degrees, or 67 degrees wingsweep positions and between Mach 0.5 and 1.0 at all altitudes and with all loads. Stick force per G does vary slightly with Mach number, stiffening up a little at supersonic speed, but remaining always in the "pleasant" category.

Opening up to max dry power, we quickly reach the Mach 0.8/500 knots IAS limit for forward-swept wing. With maneuver devices retracted, we are back to a high wing loading, low gust response ride even with the wing forward. The wing is swept manually on the Strike variant using the wing lever inboard of the throttle box. (The Air Defense variant has auto-sweep, which we would also like to see on the Strike version.) There is no trim change during sweeping and very little change of handling qualities – only a slight change in the background hum as you put the wing all the way back to 67 degrees.

The wing-mounted spoilers, which provide additional roll control with the wing forward, are switched out of circuit at sweeps greater than 50 degrees. Their effectiveness is becoming negligible at higher wing angles. The differential tail now provides both pitch and roll. But the main gain to the Strike pilot from sweeping fully back is that the wing not only attains a lower lift curve slope, but also reduces its area by about five percent as the in-board trailing edge gets tucked away into the fuselage. And now you have ride comfort in low-level turbulence that is unequaled by any other aircraft flying.

The smoothness of the ride here at 200 feet, Mach 0.92 isn't just an added tourist attraction. It makes it possible to monitor the Terrain-Following track-keeping and the HUD attack symbology without distraction or fatigue in all-weather attack conditions.

Approaching the range, let's set up for a single pass laydown attack, dropping our eight 1,000-pound bombs in a stick. With Terrain-Following selected, and Hard Ride, we can be sure that we are following the ground contours as closely as any aircraft at 600 knots can do. Wind down the "Clearance Height" setting knob to the minimum level and you are down in the weeds giving the hardest possible task to any defending weapon system. It's comforting to know that there is triplex attitude-monitoring going on in the Automatic Terrain-Following System and that you'll get an automatic pull-up before the airplane is handed back to you in the event of a failure. The only trips to date with the system have been caused by discrepancies between the different attitude sensor sensitivities, finally ironed out after many hour of TF over the Black Forest in southern Germany.

The air-to-ground weapons are selected by the navigator. Prior to flight, he can divide the stores he has to deliver into "packages" and allocate one package to each planned target. Today he has inserted one package of eight bombs in a stick at a ground spacing set in meters. As we fly toward the target, the navigator will have been monitoring the navigation system accuracy through the Combined Map and Radar Display and the TV Displays. Extensive use of Kalman Filtering ensures that navigation accuracy does not significantly degrade with time. If necessary, however, he will have updated the system through radar or laser fixing.

At about twenty miles to the target, the navigator selects the weapon package, the "Attack" mode on the TV Display, and the "Stabilized" mode on the Combined Map and Radar Display. The stabilized mode brings the computed target or radar offset to screen center overlaid with an aiming marker. An automatic radar identification tilt facility along with the stabilized mode makes the task of target identification and possible marker position refinement a low workload task.

In the front seat, you will be checking the attack progress through the HUD with hand on stick ready to take over from autopilot if you should be able to identify the target visually and see an aiming error.

As the navigator refines the target position using his own hand controller, you will notice the HUD aiming marker move to superimpose on the new target ground position and also feel the aircraft react to the autopilot adjusting the aircraft track to achieve the correct release solution. The throttles can be left alone since IAS is being controlled by the auto throttle. A circle around the aircraft symbol in the HUD unwinds to show the number of seconds to automatic bomb release. Some time before the pilot would see the target in visual conditions, the navigator will have finished aiming and the laser rangefinder will be ranging on the target position to give the weapon system very accurate plan range and aircraft height information. You will squeeze the stick-mounted pickle button, which is the pilot's "commit" signal. You can prevent release at any time up to the last second by releasing the button.

If the European weather maintains its usual form, your only contribution to the bomb drop as pilot will be to monitor the whole exercise to ensure safety. If the weather is clear, you will probably have the satisfaction of recognizing the target lying under the HUD target marker, and there is absolutely nothing to be gained by switching to a "Phase 2" attack – bringing the pilot into the loop. But if the target is seen anywhere but under the marker, or if a more attractive alternative target is seen, you can either use the "eyeball" on the hand controller to move the market accurately over the new target and let the autopilot take care of the track change required, or you can take over control of the aircraft to hand-fly to a release point, aiming with the CCIP marker (Continuously Computed Impact Point). If it's the latter case, you'll be glad that Tornado's handling qualities are so consistently excellent, because dragging an airplane out of autopilot to pull a hard turn at 200 feet and 600 knots with only two or three seconds to go to release demands nothing less.

The stick of eight 1,000-pound bombs rippling off the belly comes through as a slight shuddering and results in a noticeable acceleration, having ditched the drag. The navigator confirms all bombs gone with his Release Deficiency Indicator, and the plan would now be to stay fast and low back to where it's friendly. But today let's have a look at Tornado's handling characteristics at high Mach numbers.

The fuel system is entirely automatic, and all except the fuel in the fin is gauged. The flight refueling probe, retracted into a blister on the right side of the nose, can be used with the buddy system carried by a sister ship or with a standard tanker. But we have enough fuel remaining to briefly investigate Tornado's clean performance, giving a taste of the capabilities of the air defense variant (ADV) ordered by the RAF.

The ADV will use the Tornado's varied characteristics to achieve a different kind of sortie profile. With four semisubmerged Skyflash air-to-air missiles and two Sidewinders, it will cruise out at medium altitude and remain on combat air patrol (CAP) with wing forward. The ADV's FMICW (Frequency Modulated Interrupted Continuous Wave) radar incorporates a multi-target track-while-scan facility and gives excellent look-down performance. After high-level target contact, ADV will accelerate to a high supersonic speed, giving a capability to take out targets to altitudes well in excess of 55,000 feet, by using a combination of aircraft zoom and missile performance. Interception can be carried out "hands off" and in all weather, right down to the trees.

When approaching Mach 0.8 here at 25,000 feet, the wing is brought back to the mid 45 degree position, which compared with 67 degrees gives a reduced drag in hard maneuvering. Leading edge slat is still available at 45 degrees, but the maneuver flap is inhibited. Carefree maneuvering up to high incidence is provided courtesy of the SPILS – Spin Prevention and Incidence Limiting System. SPILS reduces roll and yaw authority at high alpha (angle of attack) and eventually limits alpha itself. The roll authority reduction is hard to detect, and very respectable roll rates are still available up to a very high incidence. The alpha limiting is felt as a "heavying up" when the limitation is approached. The system allows the pilot to get the maximum performance out of the aircraft with total confidence – a requirement that is here to stay in the modern combat aircraft.

Slamming to combat power here at 25,000 feet starts a healthy airspeed increase, and the wing is swept right back at about Mach 0.92. The 45 degree wing is, of course, good for high supersonic speeds, but we are after the optimum acceleration. There is slight Mach "noise" at Mach 0.98, but all is smooth and quiet again at the jump-up to supersonic speed and the optimum acceleration is achieved by building up to around 550 knots IAS, and then maintaining that in a climb to the tropopause. Full stick rolling here in the climb at Mach 1.5 produces only slightly lower roll rates than at the same IAS at sea level, and pitch stick forces are still very comfortable though slightly increased from their subsonic level.

The flying control system can be switched into "Mechanical" anywhere around the flight envelope, clutching in a rod linkage between stick and taileron actuators, providing a get-you-home capability in case of failure or damage. The resulting degradation in handling qualities was described (fortunately by a USAF pilot!) as making the aircraft feel "like an F-4 …" At the tropopause, our rate of Mach progress depends, of course, on the outside temperature and the aircraft's handling qualities remain good. You can put in full rudder pedal at Mach 2 – or indeed anywhere else around the flight envelope. Sideslip is automatically kept within limits, and dutch roll damping is good.

Let's cut the afterburner now and drop the nose to pick up 800 knots IAS on the way home. This is the only aircraft that the writer has flown cleared to such speeds, and surely it says all there is to say about the suitability of the airframe designed to spend most of its life hammering along at very low level. Noise levels are surprisingly low, and even at this speed the turbulence encountered on plunging through cumulus cloud comes through as very soft-edged aircraft reaction. Crew intercom is via a voice-operated switch with a dynamic switching threshold. Background noise is never sufficient in itself to switch the microphones on, and yet voice level for switching remains normal.

Airbrakes can be selected at any time, but they are scheduled to restrict their angle in relation to Mach number, and they never give an eye-pulling deceleration. They sit on the shoulders at each side of the fin and they are trim-change free. But we don't need airbrakes to decelerate from 800 knots. Idle power has the desired effect initially, and below about 600 knots the wing can be swept forward to 45 degrees, which also helps.

An experience equally impressive as smoldering along at 800 knots IAS is cruising home low level at best-range speeds. Very low fuel flows can be achieved from these fan engines, developed solely for this airframe.

The final benefit of the Tornado design to be demonstrated is also very much built-in with a war in Europe in mind. There's no doubt that a dependence on long concrete runways is going to be an embarrassment when the tanks start to roll. What's the advantage of being able to demonstrate 1,000-feet takeoff performance if it takes you 3,000 feet to stop when you get back? Let's set the aircraft up for a short landing.

Back at the home base the weather is 200 feet and a mile in rain, and we position for an Instrument Landing System (ILS) approach. The autopilot can be set to Height and Heading Hold for the final maneuvering and midflaps and gear are dropped at 300 knots and 250 knots respectively. The pattern is flown at 200 knots with "Auto Approach" selected and speed is finally bled off to 140 knots for final approach after full flap has been lowered. Full flap brings with it noticeable buffet for the first time since the bombs were dropped, but this reduces to a low level at final approach speed. The auto throttle is optimized for the approach, and IAS is kept throughout to within three knots of that selected.

The landing checklist includes a requirement to check a "Weight-on-Wheels" switch indicator before preselecting reverse thrust. Although it would need a double failure to permit airborne activation of Reverse and Lift Dump, the effects could be sobering, so the check is thought wise. With the system checked okay the throttles are rocked outboard where they continue to be moved to and fro by the auto throttle. Autopilot performance during the approach is monitored through the Head-Up Display and can be cross-checked against the raw ILS information head down. Although aircraft handling is considered ideal throughout the flight envelope, it is particularly so in the landing configuration, and visual approaches or manual ILS are equally pleasant.

At 200 feet, the runway lights appear out of the murk and the autopilot is disconnected by the thumb switch on the stick. Roundout, and as the main wheels touch down, the lift dumpers extend and kill any tendency to float. At the same time, the reverser buckets snap out on about eighty-five percent rpm and as the aircraft de-rotates, both engines are slammed to max power and the brakes are stamped on. The resulting deceleration is the nearest thing to a carrier deck landing that an air force pilot is likely to experience. In no wind, you can come to a full stop with ease in less than 1,500 feet.

As you slow through sixty knots, the re-ingestion audio warning will sound, warning you to throttle back to idle reverse to avoid reingestion. Hot gas reingestion will cause the odd pop-surge, but the real object is to avoid blowing loose stones forward and causing foreign object damage. A clean runway policy is even more important with this aircraft than usual.

Early reverse development showed up a directional stability problem at high reverse powers. Some fancy footwork was needed on the nosewheel steering to keep the aircraft on the center-line. The problem, caused by the forward jet flow attaching to the fuselage at random, was fixed in two ways. First, the reverser bucket geometry was changed to ensure engine gas-flow attachment to the upper fuselage at all times. The random yawing moments previously generated were thus eliminated. But in addition, the yaw rate signal from the CSAS was fed to the nosewheel steering system. This removed the need for pilot steering after touchdown. Now the airplane runs straight down the center-line "feet off" at max reverse.

When you shut down one engine to taxi in, the cross-drive clutch closes automatically, keeping both generators and both hydraulic pumps on line. And having canceled reverse by rocking the throttles back inboard, there is no chute to be repacked – another factor contributing to quick turnaround.

The Service Chiefs are going to be glad to see Tornado achieve mission readiness in Europe. The need for a low-level strike airplane that can operate in any weather or light conditions is clear. Of all the air-to-ground weapon systems in Europe today, Tornado has the best chance of getting through with the goods. And it's nice to know that besides being effective, the Tornado crews are going to enjoy flying it too.

Appendix 4

Flight Test Report, EAP First Flight, Warton, 8 August 1986.

The six-page flight test report for the EAP first flight at Warton on 8 August 1986.

EAP Flight number 1 – Schedule number 1 – 8th August, 1986

Results of Tests

Fuel check before start was 4,070kg: Forward 1,545kg; Rear 1,450kg; Left Wing 550kg, Right Wing 525kg.

Engine start up was made on Bus 1 to avoid RDE and selection corruptions seen previously when switching gen on Bus 2. Both engine starts were normal.

At FCS IBIT Step 38 there was already an amber lamp Reset button. The IBIT was completed and then repeated, No Go each time. The FCS was powered down on the FCS s the IBIT was repeated after repowering, and this time th was go.

There was a brief flash of L ENG NO GO on the stat while continuing with post start checks.

__Take Off__ Fuel: 3,840kg (Front 1,530kg, Rear 1,450kg, L 465kg, Right Wing 415kg). NL Governors gave 79%/79%.

The aircraft was run up to 90%NH against the brak then brakes were released while slamming to Max Reheat ation was brisk. The nose was lifted at 122 knots and aircraft flew off at about 160 knots. Pitch forces at and during the initial climb-out were slightly heavy b satisfactory. Roll response was good. The airborne a immediately felt in trim and very attitude-stable. Re cancelled very soon after lift-off to stop acceleratic knots and the gear was left down. At 210 knots, airsp height readings were compared head up and head down a within 1 knot and 100 feet. Airspeed was increased t and the Tornado chase joined for further air data com Chase airspeed and height were very close to EAP main readings. Small control inputs showed the aircraft t well damped in all three axes. Pitch response was go response excellent and yaw response much higher than quite satisfactory with familiarisation. Without co the aircraft was very attitude stable, and the immed sion was of very pleasant handling indeed, at least input envelope explored. At this low speed end of t pitch stick forces felt slightly higher than optimum

In the climb it was found that the throttles ha to very slowly close if left free.

It was noted that, although the throttles were staged together without stagger, the left engine le by about 1%NH. An incidence comparison, FTI to HUD IAS, showed FTI 6½, HUD 16.

Handling at 10,000 feet

At 10,000 feet and with gear down, airbrakes was made to 16%. At 200 knots, with fuel total 3, incidence (FTI) was 10.

- 2 -

De-classified January 1992.

B R I T I S H   A E R O S P A C E
Public Limited Company
MILITARY AIRCRAFT DIVISION
WARTON

E X P E R I M E N T A L   F L I G H T   R E P O R T

Aircraft: ZF534

Flight No.: 1	Schedule No.: 1	Date: 8th August, 1986
Pilot: J. D. Eagles	
Take-off: 15.46	Landing: 16.53	Duration: 01.07	Chock/Chock:

__TEST OBJECTIVES:__ FIRST FLIGHT

__CONFIGURATION:__ 4 Skyflash underfuselage (dummy)
2 ASRAAM outboard wing (dummy)

__TAKE-OFF LOADING:__

Total Fuel: 4,071 kg kg. Total Weight: 16,998 kg kg. Aft of Datum: 34.6% SMC

__ENGINES:__

Type: RB199 Mk.104   Serial Nos.: Left:9001 Right:9002

__SUMMARY__   Decu: Left:Bx9626 Right:Bx9611

An excellent first flight on which almost all the planned test points were covered. The only exception was individual engine handling at 30,000 feet which was cancelled after an Air Drive warning. Aircraft handling was satisfactory at all flight conditions from 140 knots IAS sea level to 1.1M, 31,000 feet.

__MODS/ALTS/CHANGES:__   Nil

__DISTRIBUTION:__

Mr. I. R. Yates
Flight Operations
Mr. J. Vincent
Mr. M. J. Walker

Mr. B. Young
Mr. R. Bedford
Mr. P. Culbert
Mr. M. D. Parry

Mr. J. M. Lowery
Mr. R. A. Hartley
Mr. P. Beckett

EAP Flight number 1 - Schedule number 1 - 8th August, 1986

At 11ʲ there was slight rumble, level 3½, from the intake area, which lasted about 3 seconds. 16° incidence FTI was achieved at 156 knots. The ADD audio warning functioned correctly at 15 degrees ADD. Handling to and at 16 ADD was stable and pleasant in all three axes. A small forward stick jerk at about 14 ADD produced the same slightly rough vibration as felt when moving the foreplane on the ground, i.e. the foreplace jack movements can be felt clearly in the cockpit if an abrupt input is made.

The aircraft was re-accelerated to 230 knots and airbrakes were extended. There was a very slight and brief kick right as airbrake was selected. Fuel was 3,340kg. The slowdown was repeated with airbrakes out to 16 ADD. Handling was identical to airbrake in except that the apparent intake rumble appeared at 14 ADD. A small yaw input at 173kt, 13 ADD showed satisfactory response and damping. Airbrake was retracted at 12 ADD.

The undercarriage was selected up at 230 kt. The undercarriage warning light sequence in the HUD and on the indicator was correct and all red lights went out cleanly after approximately 6 seconds. There was little or no mechanical noise associated with undercarriage movement. The undercarriage was lowered giving correct sequence and again about 6 seconds operation. Buffet level changed very little, i.e. the aircraft was almost completely buffet-free undercarriage up and down, at 230 knots. There was no FCS step change detectable in 1g flight with gear operation.

Brief handling checks at 250 knots gear up showed very satisfactory handling with good response in each axis and good damping.

A fuel transfer warning showed the rear pump in the right wing to be warning failure and in fact throughout the rest of the flight this nuisance warning came on as attitude affected the wing fuel sensors.

Handling at 20,000 feet

The aircraft was climbed to 20,000 feet at 280 knots and a wind up turn was made at that height at 280 knots, to 2.7g with fuel 3,000kg. Manoeuvre stability was good with the target g being easy to achieve and held accurately. Although pitch stick forces were higher than lateral, control harmony did not appear unsatisfactory.

The aircraft was accelerated at 20,000 feet to 0.9M. At 0.8M buffet level was nil and cockpit noise from the ECS was about level 3. At 0.82M, when the left engine was throttled to idle to investigate individual engine modulations, an R DRIVE warning caption lit. The left engine was reselected to Max Dry and the right pulled back to Idle. This time an L DRIVE caption appeared, followed by both L and R DRIVE together. IAS was 428kt head up and head down. When the throttles were handled together back at mid power both warnings extinguished.

- 3 -

...1 - Schedule number 1 - 8th August, 1986

...rn was made at 0.9M, 20,000 ft to 3.6g. There ...t of buffet at about 3g, accompanied by very ...oise', but handling was considered good and pitch ...found to be optimum. Fuel was 2800kg.

...0 feet

...unlight onto the displays at 30,000 feet, colour ...erately but displays were quite useable. Max ...or an acceleration. Buffet levels remained low ...le cockpit floor buffet - probably intake ...es were throttled. At 0.9M the left engine was ... No AJ was indicated and after several seconds ...ENC. The right reheat lit normally. The left ...slammed towards max reheat. This time it lit

...ly 0.95M a SENSOR failure was indicated and ...rim was required. The acceleration was ...to 1.1 Mach in a slow climb through 31,000 feet. There were no changes in attitude or handling through the Mach region, but what very slight airframe there was on the aircraft, i.e. level 2, completely disappeared around the Mach 1.0 point. Reheats were cancelled to decelerate and gentle handling as the aircraft came down through Mach 1 showed excellent response and damping. At about 0.96M there was a sudden onset of a level 3½ grinding noise from the cockpit floor area which lasted for 1 or 2 seconds and a very slight right roll tendency which was easily opposed and quickly cleared. At 0.88M with both engines throttled well back, an R DRIVE warning re-occurred and remained on when the Air Drive switch was selected to ON. The Drive was selected to OFF and this warning went out. Fuel was 2,370 kg. During the deceleration through Mach 1.0 an FCS disparity caused an amber warning on the reset button, which reset when pressed.

At 20,000 feet during descent at 0.75M, idle power, ECS was slightly noisy. When flow was selected to min, cabin flow began to oscillate at 1 to 2 Hz, but this disappeared by reselecting Max. Cabin temperature was selected to Cold and after about 5 minutes the effects of this selection were confirmed.

During descent to 5,000 feet some general handling was carried out at 300 knots with 2,300 kg fuel remaining. Handling was satisfactory. At 10,000 feet the Hunter chase formated for photography. When the aircraft was slowed to a nose-up attitude a XFER warning occurred caused by the rear wing pumps sensors uncovering.

Handling at 5,000 feet, undercarriage down

With fuel 2,100 kg, gear down, airbrake in, handling was investigated at 170 knots, (12°alpha), 1g in the following manoeuvres:

Stick jerk: Small nose down input. Good response
                       and absolutely deadbeat. The nose
                       did not tend to return at all to the
                       trimmed position.
                       - 4 -

EAP Flight number 1 – Schedule number 1 – 8th August, 1986

Longitudinal 3-2-1-1:	Satisfactory response
Lateral 3-2-1-1:	High response and satisfactory
Dutch Roll:	Good response, good damping
Steady Heading Sideslips:	Full rudder used. Approximately 15° bank needed to hold heading. Full right rudder appeared to generate more sideslip than full left.

The steady heading sideslip manoeuvres above were quite straightforward to set up. The simulator had indicated that it was difficult to control pitch attitude during this manoeuvre but this was unfounded.

The above manoeuvres were repeated at 14 ADD, airbrake in, 175 knots and at 14 ADD, airbrakes out. Handling was very similar in all cases.

A low rate barrel roll was flown at 5,000 feet, 300 knots, and was straightforward. When Max Dry power was applied at 3,000 feet a brief R LIMIT warning occurred but immediately cleared.

The aircraft was returned to base via Samlesbury and Preston. During the return and the subsequent circuit flying there were almost continuous spurious XFER warnings from wing or fuselage pumps.

Circuit Flying

An approach and overshoot was flown at a fuel state of 1,500 kg onto runway 26, W/V 280°/12 knots. The finals turn was started at 200 knots with gear down and airbrakes out. A normal approach path required 82%NH approximately and there was no sign of speed instability. Handling was excellent with the aircraft reacting slightly to small cumulus updrafts.

A final landing was made from a 12 ADD approach. 82%NH was required with a fuel state of 1,360 kg, airbrakes out. Handling remained excellent. A gentle roundout was made from about 100ft leaving power on until just before touchdown. The aircraft cushioned itself onto an extremely soft touchdown. Lateral control at roundout was slightly touchy. The stick was moved forward for derotation and again the nosewheel touchdown could not be felt due to the very soft nose oleo. The drag chute was selected after derotation and deployed after about 3 seconds. Lift Dump was manually selected at 112 knots. The parachute was very effective but Lift Dump effect could not be detected in either drag or pitch. Only moderate wheel braking was required to stop once speed was reduced to about 50 knots. In dispersal, I.N. groundspeed was 1 knot.

Other Observations

Trim Rates

In the air, roll trim rate appeared high but satisfactory using a 'blip' technique. Pitch trim was slower and satisfactory.

Schedule 1 – 8th August, 1986

...actory temperature control but flow pulsing ...t max flow. The system was slightly noisy ...ceptable.

...in the circuit was very satisfactory at ...however, appeared high and higher ...ly useable.

...irst flight with an aircraft that quickly ...ts strong attitude stability and easy ...eral lack of buffet even with gear down was impressive. Only intake spillage noise when throttling back, and a moderate foreplane actuator noise/vibration when making sharp pitch inputs, detracted from a very smooth and quiet aircraft. Both of these were of minor effect and quite acceptable. Performance was noticeably better than Tornado off the runway and slightly better than Tornado during airborne accelerations, even with leading edge slat fixed out. Circuit handling was simple, and clearly the aircraft will permit early power bleed and a strong roundout to bring touchdown speeds down.

An impressive first flight that reflects credit on the whole design team.

Defects

1. Left reheat lit at 0.9M/30,000' but would not stage – gave ENC on cancellation. Subsequent slam selection OK.

2. Throttles tend to fall back towards idle in 1g flight.

3. DDVR warning after only 7 minutes flight.

4. Fuel transfer warning at nose up attitudes.

5. "L DRIVE" when right engine was throttled back at 0.90M, 30,000' and vice versa. Later, with engines matched at 0.88M at idle, "R DRIVE" warning.

6. R LIMIT warning when engines were slammed to Max Dry, 1,000', 350 kts.

7. 'SENS' warning at 0.98M during acceleration.

All the above snags were acceptable for further flight.

J. D. EAGLES
EXECUTIVE DIRECTOR, FLIGHT OPERATIONS

Appendix 5

Note to the board members of DASA. Ottobrun, Munich, October 1996.

'Test Pilot Involvement in Engineering'

The major Aerospace Companies such as Aerospatiale, Alenia, BAe, Boeing, DASA, Dassault, and so on, all employ on their staff, qualified test pilots as part of their teams. By "qualified" I mean pilots who have graduated from one of the recognised Schools such as EPNR, ETPS, NTPS, USAFTPS or the USNTPS. The schools teach test flying techniques of course; in other words the methods of safely gathering the data that manufacturers and customers need in order to assess the performance and handling characteristics of an aircraft and its systems. But in addition to teaching these techniques, the schools teach all the classic disciplines involved in the business, like Aerodynamics, Stability and Control, Electronics, Human Engineering, Systems, Structures, etc. The purpose is not to attempt to make the pilot an expert in these fields, but to teach him enough of the subject and the language to enable him to talk to the expert and hopefully understand and be understood. The pilot is then potentially able to contribute much more to the Company's aims than only flying the aircraft under test.

However, the degree to which the different Companies encourage their pilots to contribute in these non-flying areas has varied widely over the years and has depended very much on the character and personality of the senior engineering executives involved and of the pilots themselves. Some Technical Directors and Heads of Departments in these Companies have actually deliberately excluded the Flight Operations people from getting involved in "their" business until the aircraft or system is ready for flying. One memorable character, when asked by a Chief Test Pilot if he could send his Project Pilot to an early meeting on a new fighter, said "When the cart is ready, we'll send for the horse"! But after noting the amount of pilot involvement in Engineering Departments in many of those Companies over the years, I have absolutely no doubt that early pilot contribution is essential if the Company is to "get it right first time".

The warmth with which the test pilots are welcomed into engineering areas also depends a good deal on the character of the pilots themselves. Inevitably, some of them, during their colourful careers, tend to adopt a God-like attitude towards their fellow mortals. A "Who was in charge here before I arrived" sort of position. And probably all test pilots when fresh out of test pilot school have a burning desire to "tell it like it is" and leave no rivet unturned in their critical report on the aircraft or system they are called upon to assess. They feel they have made a sort of Hippocratic oath to insist on only the best for the pilot profession. All of this tends to lead to the engineers adopting as the first rule of their trade: "Don't invite the opposition to the meeting". What are we to do about all this?

Firstly we have to recognise the value, the essential need, in getting the pilots (and navigators in appropriate projects) involved from the very beginning. There are many horror stories of elements of an aircraft design being based on incorrect assumptions which a test pilot would probably have questioned even at the early discussion stages. The ones I am familiar with would all come under the heading of "Company Confidential"! And it also must be said that a past Air Force pilot or current private pilot on the engineering staff is no substitute for the involvement of the Company test pilot. The presence of retired or private pilots within projects is an excellent thing and often serves to eliminate some of the more obvious misconceptions. In the good old days of seemingly unlimited funding, Aircraft Companies occasionally paid for flying training for some of their engineering staff to introduce some of this general experience into their thinking. But today the business is so specialised and so sensitive in cost terms to any shortfall in design quality, that we are crazy to proceed with any project without scrutinising it at all stages with the best professional eyes we have available in our Company. And our Company test pilots are trained to do just that.

So that brings us to the part the pilots have to play. Psychology comes into the picture here. Test pilots are critics, and nobody loves a critic. When a designer finds the system he has been working on for the last 2 years, being criticised by some 30 year old wizz kid, he has a natural tendency to defend his system and to dislike the test pilot. (The situation is even more explosive if the test pilot fraternity were not brought into the process during those

2 years of design). The pilot must never allow his position as a professional critic to overshadow his place as a member of the Company team. That is not to say that he should not assess and criticise; that's what he is paid to do. But he must make every effort to get involved in the early engineering stages of the business to ensure as far as possible that there will be no unwelcome surprises when the various systems come up for flight-testing. And of course he must deliver his messages with diplomacy.

The test pilot must not only make his assessment in relation to the absolute ideal, he must also clearly understand the customer specification to which the system was designed. In an ideal world, the pilot would have attended the meeting at which the customer presented his specification and would have commented at that stage on any deviation between the requirement and his idea of the absolute ideal. And he would then have stayed close to the designer through all stages of the design, including mock-up and rig work. Then there would probably be few surprises when the system was finally flown. In reality of course, the pilot would not be continuously available but if the designer calls well planned meetings at appropriate stages, our goal of getting it right first time is made more probable.

Apart from those areas where flight safety is involved, the pilot has to learn, like all the rest of us in the business, that "the best is the enemy of the good". That achieving 98 per cent of the requirement with 100 per cent of the effort/funding, is better than achieving 99 or 100 per cent of the requirement with 150 per cent of the effort/funding. And here the Company is best served if the pilot gives his 'absolute' view to the engineering department and then accepts their assessment of what steps to take next. If the decision is to offer the system to the customer with characteristics which the test pilot would prefer to see changed, that is the Company's prerogative and the pilot must accept it and support that situation. It follows of course that Engineering must have that meeting with the pilot at which the subject can be discussed without the customer present. If this process of establishing a "Company Line" is not established, we will see Company test pilot and Customer test pilot joining forces against Company Engineering at the final assessment meeting. And that is another cause for Engineering to exclude the test pilot from further involvement.

Here in DASA there is a decided lack of pilot involvement in the early stages of engineering projects. The distance between Ottobrun and Manching is one major reason, but another is the fact that the need for this involvement is not ingrained in our company culture. We have got to change that. It isn't possible to quantify the cost of not having this element in our process but it must be clear to see that such involvement must increase our chances of avoiding change at a late and expensive time in the project. To bring this about the pilots must get used to more travel between Flight Operations at Manching and Engineering in Ottobrun. They are happy to do that within the time they have available. But the key element is that the engineering sections involved should recognise the need and call the meetings. If in doubt, engineers should get used to calling the project pilot or Chief Test Pilot at Manching to discuss the subject with him and to determine whether a pilot input would be helpful.

J.D. E.
Director Flight Test
October 1996